The Healing Power of God

Releasing the Power of the Holy Spirit

By: Bill Vincent

The Healing Power of GodLULUjacket

© 2016 by Bill Vincent.
All rights reserved. No part of this book may be reproduced, stored in a retrieval system or transmitted in any form or by any means without the prior written permission of the publishers, except by a reviewer who may quote brief passages in a review to be printed in a newspaper, magazine or journal.

Paperback: 978-1-60796-981-5

PUBLISHED BY REVIVAL WAVES OF GLORY BOOKS & PUBLISHING
www.revivalwavesofgloryministries.com
Litchfield, IL
Printed in the United States of America

The Healing Power of GodLULUjacket

Table of Contents

Book Disclaimer 4
Introduction 5
Important Points 6
Faith and Healing 12
Speak with Authority 20
The Proof is in the Bible 29
How to Lay Hands on the Sick 30
Using this Technique 41
Carpal Tunnel Technique 44
Casting Out Demons 45
Diseases and Afflictions 50
What If Someone Doesn't Get Healed? 66
Continuing Study 70
Healing Faith 71
Healing is God's Will 73
Already Been Paid For 76
Doubt, and Unbelief Can Hinder Your Faith 79
Receiving Your Healing 83
Conclusion 96
About the Author 98
Recommended Books 99

Book Disclaimer

Here are tips on reading Bill Vincent's Books.

Bill writes prophetically as God speaks. The grammar may be pushed but the message is spoken from the heart of God. Bill didn't want to lose the depth of revelation through extensive editing.

Introduction

The purpose of this Book is to present some important principles of healing which may help you as you step out in faith and begin laying hands on the sick.

The information in this Book might be different than what you have always been taught, but consider keeping an open mind in case God wants to reveal something new to you. Check these things against the Bible; don't just believe what I say or what other people have said!

Important Points

It's time to see Healings and Miracles today. Christians have the authority to lay hands on the sick and cast out demons.

We receive *dunamis*, the miracle-working power of the Holy Spirit, when we receive the baptism of the Holy Spirit after we become Christians. Here is a simple prayer for receiving the baptism of the Holy Spirit: "Lord Jesus, You said in (Luke 11:13) that as a child of God I can ask for the gift of the Holy Spirit. You also said in (Acts 1:4-8) that I will receive power when I am baptized with the Holy Spirit.

So Lord, I am asking in Your Name, the Name of Jesus, for You to baptize me in the Holy Spirit right now, exactly like on the day of Pentecost. I might not feel any different, but I receive the gift of the power of the Holy Spirit right now, by my faith. Thank You, Lord! Amen."

If you sincerely prayed this prayer in faith, then believe that you have received the power of the Holy Spirit for carrying out the Great Commission. This means that you now have the ability to pray in tongues and hear what the Holy Spirit is saying.

I urge you to begin praying in tongues every day, but it is likely that you can now lay hands on people and see miraculous healings even if you have not yet begun exercising your new ability to pray in tongues.

The main purpose for miracles is to point people to Jesus. (see John 10:25, 37-38, 12:37, 14:11 and 20:30-31.)

Always remember that the glory goes to God, so don't accept any glory for yourself.

What about the belief of sicknesses, diseases, and injuries and so on is not "crosses" that we must bear. Let's look at what Jesus said about this: "And He said to all, If any person wills to come after Me, let him deny himself - that is, disown himself, forget, lose sight of himself and his own interests, refuse and give up himself - and *take up his cross daily* and follow Me [that is, cleave steadfastly to Me, conform wholly to My example, in living and if need be in dying also]."
(Luke 9:23, AMP)

Notice what it means to "take up our cross." In the Amplified Version of the Bible (which tries to provide the shades of meaning from the original Greek), Jesus said that we must lose sight of ourselves and our interests and give up our own desires, plans, goals, ambitions and opinions.

"Taking up our cross" means that we must follow Jesus' example and be "dead to self," as the apostle Paul described it: "I have been *crucified* with Christ and *I no longer live*, but Christ lives in me." (Galatians 2:20)

For example, notice that Jesus denied Himself His own interests and ambitions and He only did what the Father told Him to do: "Jesus gave them this answer: "I tell you the truth, *the Son can do nothing by himself*; he can do *only* what he sees his Father doing, because *whatever the Father does the Son also does*." (John 5:19)

"*By myself I can do nothing*; I judge *only as I hear* and my judgment is just, for *I seek not to please myself but him who sent me*." (John 5:30)

So Jesus said, "When you have lifted up the Son of Man, then you will know that I am the one I claim to be and that *I do nothing on my own but speak just what the Father has taught me."* (John 8:28)

"Don't you believe that I am in the Father and that the Father is in me? *The words I say to you are not just my own. Rather, it is the Father, living in me, who is doing his work."* (John 14:10)

The cross does not represent burdens that we must carry (as many people believe), the cross is a place of *death*. The Bible tells us to *die* to our "self" nature (any attitudes, decisions, motives, etc., which do not line up with God's plans and timing), just as Jesus did. "Bearing our cross" does not refer to being sick or having crippling diseases or injuries.

When Jesus was ruthlessly tortured and brutally executed, He purchased not only our salvation but also our healing.

For example, the prophet Isaiah said that Jesus would take up our infirmities, carry our sorrows, be pierced for our transgressions, be crushed for our iniquities, be punished for our peace and be wounded for our healing: "Surely he *took up our infirmities* and *carried our sorrows*, yet we considered him stricken by God, smitten by him and afflicted. But he was *pierced for our transgressions*, he was *crushed for our iniquities*; the *punishment that brought us peace* was upon him, and *by his wounds we are healed."* (Isaiah 53:4-5)

Christians tend to believe the salvation parts of this prophecy which were fulfilled when Jesus died for our sins, but we must not simply focus on the parts of Scripture that we like and ignore the parts that we're not comfortable with.

If the salvation parts of Isaiah's prophecy apply to us (and they do) then the healing parts of his prophecy apply to us as well. (Isaiah 53:4-5) plainly states that Jesus would bear our sins (purchasing our salvation) and that He would bear our sicknesses (purchasing our healing).

Notice that Jesus paid for our *sins* 2000 years ago, yet sinners are not automatically forgiven. They must *receive* forgiveness of sins by faith (Acts 26:18). Healing works in a similar way, because Jesus paid for our *healing* 2000 years ago, yet we must *receive* healing by faith (Luke 18:42). When we lay hands on people, we can believe for them to be healed when faith is present (just as we receive salvation by faith) because Jesus has already paid for the healing.

Christians sometimes ask, "*Why do we need to lay hands on the sick? I believe that God can heal people when we pray for them.*"

Prayer is extremely important, there is no doubt about that and God sometimes does heal people when we pray for them. But you see, that isn't the issue. The issue is that Jesus has commanded us to fulfill the Great Commission by continuing His earthly ministry until He returns for us at the end of the age. This means that we are meant to share the Good News with people, *lay hands on the sick* and cast out demons.

In (Luke 4:40), for example, the people brought to Jesus *all* who were sick. Certainly Jesus could have snapped His fingers and healed all of them in an instant, right? But He didn't. The verse says, "*laying his hands on each one*, he healed them."

It probably took a long time for Him to lay hands on every one of those sick people, but laying hands on the sick is one of the main methods that God has chosen for divine healing. Therefore, Jesus had to be obedient and so do we. In fact, sick people often specifically begged Jesus to lay His *hands* on them because they knew that He often healed by the method of the laying-on of hands (see Matthew 9:18 and

Mark 8:22, for example). In the original Greek, (Acts 5:12) says that signs and wonders were done "through the *hands of the apostles*" (see for example the Amplified Version and the King James Version). (Hebrews 6:1-2) tells us that *the laying-on of hands* was an elementary, foundational teaching for new Christians. (John 14:11-12) says that believers will do the *same* miracles that Jesus did, which includes laying *hands* on the sick. (Mark 16:17-18) says that believers will *place their hands on sick people* and they will get well.

Why do we need to lay hands on people? Simply because Jesus told us to do that (Mark 16:18 and John 14:12). If Jesus had commanded us to heal people in some other way then that is the way we would need to do it. Our job is to be obedient to our Master, not to question His judgment!

Another question that people sometimes ask is, "*Why do you say that I have to speak in tongues in order to lay hands on the sick?*"

Well, it's not so much that you have to speak in tongues in order to lay hands on people, it's just that speaking in tongues is the usual, Scriptural evidence that you have received the baptism of the Holy Spirit.

Jesus specifically said that the power of the Holy Spirit is imparted to us when we are baptized with the Holy Spirit.

Speaking in tongues does not necessarily happen *automatically* when we receive the baptism of the Holy Spirit because we must choose to open our mouths and speak. Plus, our analytical minds do not like to give up control and allow us to speak out words that are coming from our spirits and this makes it difficult for many people when they try to pray in tongues for the first time. For this reason, I personally believe that people can receive this Spirit baptism, whether immediately after they are saved or at a later time, without actually saying anything in tongues right away.

They have the *ability* to pray in tongues, but they don't know that they have this ability (due to wrong teaching) or else they don't quite know how to speak out words which are coming from their spirits. For example, I led my mom through a prayer to receive the baptism of the Holy Spirit, but she was not able to get her mind out of the way enough to allow the words to come up out of her spirit in tongues. However, my mom has laid hands on people and they have been healed. So I personally feel that my mom has received the baptism of the Holy Spirit and has the ability to pray in tongues in the Scriptural manner, but she had not done it yet.

Praying in tongues is the *usual* outward evidence that we have been baptized with the Holy Spirit, but I believe that a person can receive this baptism without speaking in tongues right then and there.

I would suggest that you lay hands on the sick in faith no matter what your view of tongues happens to be. But if God is not confirming His Word for you by healing people, consider that it might be because you haven't received the baptism of the Holy Spirit with the (usual) evidence of speaking in tongues, because Jesus said you would receive *power* when you receive this baptism.

Faith and Healing

There is a major need for faith for healing. This is a fresh take on faith and healing. First of all, notice that Jesus was *hindered* from doing miracles when there was a lack of faith: "When the Sabbath came, he began to teach in the synagogue and many who heard him were amazed. "Where did this man get these things?" they asked. "What's this wisdom that has been given him that he even does miracles! Isn't this the carpenter? Isn't this Mary's son and the brother of James, Joseph, Judas and Simon? Aren't his sisters here with us?" And they took offense at him.

Jesus said to them, "Only in his hometown, among his relatives and in his own house is a prophet without honor."

He could not do any miracles there, except lay his hands on a few sick people and heal them. And he was amazed at their *lack of faith*. (Mark 6:2-6)

The above passage tells us that a few individual people received healing in Jesus' hometown, but otherwise Jesus was *unable* to do miracles there because of their lack of faith! (Also see Matthew 13:58). The Greek word for "able" in this passage essentially means "To be able" (*The Complete Word Study Dictionary of the New Testament*, Spiros Zodhiates, p.485) and it is used in a negative sense in this passage ("not able").

We can see in the Gospel of Mark that Jesus did miracles both before and after (Mark 6:2-6 above), so it is reasonable to assume that Jesus still had the power to do miracles while He was in His hometown.

Then why was He "not able" to do miracles in His hometown, other than laying hands on a few people? A prominent Bible commentary puts it this way: "Because of such persistent unbelief Jesus could not do any miracles there except to lay His hands on a few sick people and heal them. *There was no limitation on His power, but His purpose was to perform miracles in the presence of faith.* Only a few here had faith to come to Him for healing." (*The Bible Knowledge Commentary*, Walvoord and Zuck, Dallas Theological Seminary, p.127, emphasis added).

In other words, Jesus certainly had the *power* to do miracles in His hometown, but He did not force His power to work in people who were unwilling to receive it. Because of such persistent unbelief in His hometown, Jesus could not do any miracles there.

In (Mark 5:22-43), a synagogue ruler named Jairus asked Jesus to heal his dying daughter. As Jesus was on His way to Jairus' house, a woman who had been subject to bleeding for twelve years touched Jesus' cloak and was instantly healed. Notice *how* she was healed: [Jesus] said to her, "Daughter, *your faith has healed you*." (Mark 5:34)

Jesus said that it was *her faith* which had healed her. Now, after this woman was healed, Jairus (the synagogue ruler) learned that his daughter had died.

Notice that Jesus *ignored* the "bad report" and told Jairus to *believe* and not to fear: "While Jesus was still speaking, some men came from the house of Jairus, the synagogue ruler. "Your daughter is dead," they said. "Why bother the teacher any more?"

Ignoring what they said, Jesus told the synagogue ruler, "*Don't be afraid; just believe*." (Mark 5:35-36)

Jesus immediately disputed the "bad report" that people had spoken and He told Jairus to continue to have *faith*. When Jesus arrived at Jairus' house, He was confronted by people who were speaking doubt and unbelief, so what did He do? He *cleared the room* of all those doubters: "When they came to the home of the synagogue ruler, Jesus saw a commotion, with people crying and wailing loudly.

He went in and said to them, "Why all this commotion and wailing? The child is not dead but asleep." But *they laughed at him*. After he *put them all out*, he took the child's father and mother and the disciples who were with him and went in where the child was.

He took her by the hand and said to her, "Talitha cumi!" (which means, "Little girl, I say to you, get up!"). Immediately the girl stood up and walked around (she was twelve years old). (Mark 5:38-42)

So even though Jesus had infinite faith, we can see that healings and miracles depended to some degree on the faith (or lack of faith) of other people.

In the next few passages, notice that the miracles happened *because of* people's faith: "Jesus said to him, "*Receive* your sight; *your faith has healed you*." Immediately he *received* his sight and followed Jesus, praising God." (Luke 18:42-43)

As he was going into a village, ten men who had leprosy met him. They stood at a distance and called out in a loud voice, "Jesus, Master, have pity on us!"

When he saw them, he said, "*Go, show yourselves to the priests*." And *as they went*, they were cleansed. One of them, when he saw he was healed, came back, praising God in a loud voice. He threw himself at Jesus' feet and thanked him--and he was a Samaritan. Jesus asked, "Were not all ten cleansed? Where are the other nine? Was no one found to return and give praise to God except this foreigner?" Then he said to him, "Rise and go; *your faith has made you well.*" (Luke 17:12-19)

As Jesus went on from there, two blind men followed him, calling out, "Have mercy on us, Son of David!" When he had gone indoors, the blind men came to him and he asked them, "*Do you believe* that I am able to do this?" "Yes, Lord," they replied.

Then he touched their eyes and said, "*According to your faith will it be done to you*"; and their sight was restored. (Matthew 9:27-30)

"Some men brought to him a paralytic, lying on a mat. When Jesus *saw their faith*, he said to the paralytic, "Take heart, son; your sins are forgiven." At this point, some of the teachers of the law said to themselves, "This fellow is blaspheming!" Knowing their thoughts, Jesus said, "Why do you entertain evil thoughts in your hearts? Which is easier: to say, 'Your sins are forgiven,' or to say, 'Get up and walk'?

But so that you may know that the Son of Man has authority on earth to forgive sins. . . ." Then he said to the paralytic, "*Get up*, take your mat and go home." *And the man got up* and went home. (Matthew 9:2-7)

"*By faith* in the name of Jesus, this man whom you see and know was made strong. It is Jesus' name *and the faith* that comes through him that has given this complete healing to him, as you can all see." (Acts 3:16)

"In Lystra there sat a man crippled in his feet, who was lame from birth and had never walked. He listened to Paul as he was speaking. Paul looked directly at him, *saw that he had faith to be healed* and called out, "Stand up on your feet!" At that, *the man jumped up* and began to walk." (Acts 14:8-10)

In several of these passages, Jesus said, "*Your faith* has healed you," or "*According to your faith* will it be done to you." In a couple of instances, Jesus and the apostles *saw* that a person had faith to be healed. Several passages say that the people *received* their healing by their actions of faith.

Now, what if these people did *not* have faith? What if the lame or paralyzed people in these passages had refused to get up on their feet? After all, it must have sounded ridiculous when Jesus or the apostles commanded a lame person to get up onto his feet when obviously his legs did not work properly! What if the man in (Matthew 12:13) had refused to stretch out his shriveled hand? What if the lame man at the pool of Bethesda in (John 5:2-9) had refused to get up when Jesus told him to?

What if all of these people had reacted with doubt and unbelief and said things like, "What do you mean, 'Get up'? Can't you see I'm lame" If these people had not put their faith into action then they would not have received their healing. After all, Jesus repeatedly told people, "*Your faith* has healed you," or "*According to your faith* will it be done to you."

As you read the Gospels, notice that Jesus sometimes *measured* people's faith. He said things like, "You of *little* faith," or "I have not found such *great* faith even in Israel," or "Be it done *according to your faith*," and so on. If you examine closely all of the miracles that Jesus did, you'll find that there were often actions of faith which were performed by other people.

For example, we tend to say that *Jesus* turned the water into wine at the wedding at Cana in Galilee (John 2:1-10), but that is not entirely accurate. Recall that the servants *knew* that they had put water into the six stone water jars, yet Jesus told them to take some of that water to the master of the banquet as if it was really wine! Jesus' miracles frequently required an action of faith on someone's part.

In fact, the *greater* the faith that was demonstrated, the greater the miracles that resulted. For example, there are two events in the New Testament in which Jesus said that someone had *great* faith (Matthew 8:5-13 and Matthew 15:22-28). In *both* cases, Jesus healed a person *at a distance*. Jesus did not need to see the sick person or touch the person or talk to the person or anything. Why?

Because someone demonstrated *great* faith. There is only one other time that Jesus healed someone at a distance in the Gospels and the Bible says that "*The man took Jesus at his word* and departed. While he was still on the way, his servants met him with the news that his boy was living." (John 4:50-51).

Again, someone demonstrated great faith by taking Jesus at His word and a person was healed at a distance.

Now that we understand that faith plays such a big role in healing, this gives us some insight into other healing passages in the Gospels. For example, (Matthew 14:35-36) says that people begged Jesus to let the sick just touch the edge of His cloak so that they would be healed. Why did Jesus allow them to touch His cloak? Why didn't He simply lay His hands on them?

They had *faith* that they would be healed if they touched Jesus' cloak, so He allowed them to put their faith into *action* and they were healed.

This might also explain why Jesus did some strange-sounding things in order to heal several people: "There were people brought to him, a man who was deaf and could hardly talk and they begged him to place his hand on the man. After he *took him aside, away from the crowd*, Jesus put his fingers into the man's ears.

Then he *spit and touched the man's tongue*. He looked up to heaven and with a deep sigh said to him, "Ephphatha!" (which means, "Be opened!"). At this point, the man's ears were opened, his tongue was loosened and he began to speak plainly." (Mark 7:32-35)

"They came to Bethsaida, and some people brought a blind man and begged Jesus to touch him. He took the blind man by the hand and *led him outside the village*. When he had *spit on the man's eyes* and put his hands on him, Jesus asked, "Do you see anything?" He looked up and said, "I see people; they look like trees walking around." Once more Jesus put his hands on the man's eyes. Then his eyes were opened, his sight was restored, and he saw everything clearly." (Mark 8:22-25)

"Having said this, he *spit on the ground, made some mud with the saliva, and put it on the man's eyes*. "Go," he told him, "wash in the Pool of Siloam" (this word means Sent). So the man went and washed, and came home seeing." (John 9:6-7)

Jesus is the Son of God, so why did He spit in people's eyes and make mud with His saliva and so on? Surely His power is so great that He didn't really need to do those things, right? Well, consider that it is not just Jesus' great power and His great faith and His great authority that brings healing, because we have seen over and over that people's *faith* sometimes played a role in their healing.

When Jesus took these people away from the crowd, when He spit into their eyes, when He made mud from His saliva and so on, these were probably not necessary for increasing Jesus' power or His faith, right? But they might have been factors for increasing *the deaf and blind people's* faith.

Based on all of these Scriptural examples of how healing works, you will probably see greater results when there is greater faith present. You can build faith in people by showing them the Scriptural proof that healing is "for today," by telling people about some of the other healings you have witnessed, by having them watch other people get healed, by asking them about their theological problems concerning healing or their doubts and fears about healing, and so on.

In the New Testament, people put their faith into action and *then* they were healed and the same principle holds true today. Many times you will find that after you command healing in a person's back, for example, the healing will manifest itself when the person begins to move around and bend his back, putting his faith into action.

I still have a lot to learn about the connection between faith and healing (for example, atheists sometimes get healed even though they have *no* faith!).

Speak with Authority

If you want to see God heal the sick speak with authority. You don't have to yell for people to receive but you need to speak with authority. Always speak with *authority* when commanding healing to take place. Say it like you mean it!

The dictionary defines an ambassador as a person who is the highest-ranking representative appointed by one government to represent it to another government. An ambassador is an official agent who speaks on behalf of the government he is representing, with the full authority and backing and power of that government. The apostle Paul said: "*we* are *Christ's ambassadors*" (2 Corinthians 5:20, AMP)

"Clothe yourselves therefore, as (*God's own picked representatives,*) His own *chosen ones*" (Colossians 3:12, AMP)

You are an ambassador or an agent of Jesus Christ on this earth, His own chosen, hand-picked representative! When you command healing in His Name you are doing it on His behalf, with the full authority and backing and power of the Lord Jesus Christ. Speak with *authority* when you speak in His Name, because the Name of Jesus is above the name of every disease and every demon! When an FBI agent confidently flashes his badge, he expects immediate respect and usually he gets it. When you flash the Name of Jesus at the enemy, *expect* the devil or the sickness to flee!

Notice that speaking with authority does not mean shouting. Have you ever been in a store and heard a parent whisper forcefully to a misbehaving child, "Get over here *right now!*"

It might not have been loud enough for anyone else to hear, but the child knew he'd better get over there right away. That is speaking with authority.

Jesus healed people in different ways; He did not stick to a single formula. We must always try to be sensitive to the leading of the Holy Spirit when laying hands on the sick. The Holy Spirit is the Teacher and He never stops teaching those who are eager and willing to learn and willing to *do* what they are taught. Don't expect the Holy Spirit to teach you new things if you aren't willing to *do* what He teaches you!

The apostle John said that the whole world would not have room for the books that could be written about the things Jesus did (John 21:25).

Since we don't know everything Jesus did, we need to try different things in order to get the sick person healed, following the *principles* given in Scripture. The purpose of this Healing Book is to give you some ideas on how to do this.

If one thing doesn't work and the person isn't getting healed, ask God to give you discernment and then try something else (as we will see in Part Four of these handouts). Be *persistent*, because God honors persistence (see Luke 11:5-10).

You need to *believe* and *know* that you have been called to do the supernatural in your daily life, because that is exactly what Jesus told us to do in the Great Commission.

You also need to believe without a shadow of a doubt that Jesus lives His life *in you* and *through you*. Jesus laid His hands on people while He was on the earth, but then He took His hands with Him when He ascended back into heaven. Now He lives *in you*, you are His hands and feet on the earth! Wherever you go, Jesus goes with you. Whatever you touch, Jesus touches. When you lay hands on someone,

Jesus within you is laying hands on the person as well. Step out in faith and *believe* that people are going to be healed. *Expect* it and you will see awesome miracles which will bring many people to Christ. Nothing is impossible for Jesus in you!

Notice that when you flip a light switch you *expect* the light to come on.

It is possible that the light bulb is burned out, but since this doesn't happen very often you don't have to work up a bunch of faith before flipping the switch, you simply turn on the light with complete *expectation* that the light will come on. The same principle works with healing. You don't need to try to work up a bunch of faith before laying hands on someone, just do it with the *expectation* that it will work. This level of expectation will build in you as you gain more experience in laying hands on the sick. Nobody knows everything about how healing works, just as most of us don't know everything about how electricity works. But we can still turn on a light switch!

We can use electricity without understanding everything about it and we can heal the sick without having all of our questions answered.

Keep your eyes open when you lay hands on the sick so that you don't miss the miracles! Tell the person you are laying hands on not to act "religious" by closing his eyes or frowning seriously (as many people will tend to do), tell him to smile and relax and keep his eyes open so that he can watch his arm or leg grow out or his tumors fall off or his bones straighten out or whatever the need happens to be. Don't miss watching the miracles happen and don't miss seeing the person's eyes bulge out with joy when he is instantly and miraculously healed!

When the power of God goes into someone, it occasionally causes the person to fall to the ground (usually backwards).

Try to make sure that there is nothing behind the person that he might fall onto, or better yet try to have someone behind him to catch him and gently lower him to the ground. The frail human body sometimes reacts this way when the awesome power of God goes into it and sometimes God uses a "divine anesthetic" (so to speak) as He heals people, just as He did for Adam (Genesis 2:21).

Your beliefs might not allow for such things as "falling out under the power of God," but keep this point in mind anyway because God is God and He isn't going to squeeze Himself into the little boxes that we keep trying to put Him in. As you lay hands on people, some of them might fall out under the power of God (and some people might fall just because they think they're supposed to!), so be sensitive to this possibility as you minister healing.

Jesus laid His hands on the eyes of blind people (Matthew 9:28-30), He put His fingers in the ears of deaf people (Mark 7:33), He touched the tongues of mute people (Mark 7:33) and so on. It is often best to lay your hands as close as possible to the afflicted area so that the power of the Holy Spirit is directed right to the source of the problem.

Use wisdom and common sense, though. If the problem is in an area where your hands have no business being, ask the person to put his own hand near the area and then you can put your hand on his hand. Also, don't touch an open sore because you are living in a physical body which is susceptible to catching diseases.

Yes, you can then lay hands on yourself and you might get healed, but why risk it? Just because you heal the sick every day, it doesn't mean that you'll never catch the flu, it doesn't mean that you'll never have to wear glasses, it doesn't mean that you'll never go bald and so on. Even if you are sick, though, you can still lay hands on people and they can still be healed (just make sure that you wash your hands and that you don't cough in their faces!). Your physical health has no bearing on your authority to lay hands on the sick because Jesus within you never gets sick.

Jesus came so that we might have life, and have it to the full (John 10:10), but the devil (the thief) comes only to steal and kill and destroy (John 10:10). The devil will try to sow seeds of doubt to make people think they didn't get healed.

He knows that we must *believe* that we have received healing: "I tell you the truth, if anyone says to this mountain, 'Go, throw yourself into the sea,' and *does not doubt* in his heart but *believes* that what he says will happen, it will be done for him. Therefore I tell you, whatever you ask for in prayer, *believe that you have received it, and it will be yours.*" (Mark 11:23-24)

The devil knows this Scripture just as well as you do, so he knows that all he has to do is to put doubts and fears in people's minds. This can prevent the healing from happening and it can sometimes cause a person to *lose* his healing if he gives in to doubts.

As Christians, we are meant to live by faith, not by sight (2 Corinthians 5:7). Don't be moved by what you see, hear, think, feel, taste, touch, or smell.

We are easily fooled by our senses and the devil can use our physical senses to deceive us. Stand on what the Word of God says and live by faith, not by sight. In other words, don't be intimidated by the physical problems that people might have, because God can heal anything!

When a person receives healing, explain that the devil will sometimes put *symptoms* back on a person in order to create doubt in the healing power of God. There have been many examples of people who were instantly healed, but within a day or two they noticed that the pain or symptoms had returned. Fortunately some of them were aware that this might happen, so they simply told the devil to get out in the Name of Jesus and the pain or symptoms instantly vanished. This has happened several times to people after someone laid hands on them.

I urge you to tell the devil sternly, "Devil, you can just take that right back because *I'm not signing for that package!*" and the pain will instantly leave! This has happened over and over.

When healing people, it is essential that we do not tell them to stop taking their medications or anything like that. First of all it would be considered practicing medicine without a license, which is illegal. Secondly, the Bible tells us to obey the authorities and therefore when a person submits to the authority of a doctor then he should obey that doctor. Always tell people to continue their medication and to go to their doctor as soon as possible in order to be pronounced healthy by the doctor.

It does not display a lack of faith to go to a doctor. For one thing, if a person doesn't get healed when you lay hands on him then it can be very helpful to find out the specific medical diagnosis so that you can use that information to get the person healed.

Jesus and the apostles were often ridiculed by religious people and they were accused of doing demonic things. This is also true today. When you step out in faith and begin laying hands on the sick in obedience to the Great Commission, expect to be ridiculed. Ironically, atheists don't care about the healing power of God because they don't believe in God in the first place, so it will be your own brothers and sisters in Christ who will ridicule you and accuse you of doing things which are "of the devil" (speaking in tongues and so on).

Love them anyway and don't let this deter you, because *blessed* are you when people ridicule you for the obedient works that you are doing in His Name (Matthew 5:11 and Luke 6:23).

Keep in mind that our goal must always be to please God. We must not disobey God out of a fear of being rejected by friends or family or brothers or sisters in Christ: "Do not suppose that I have come to bring peace to the earth. I did not come to bring peace, but a sword. For I have come to turn a man *against* his father, a daughter *against* her mother, a daughter-in-law *against* her mother-in-law-- *a man's enemies will be the members of his own household."*

Anyone who loves his father or mother *more* than me *is not worthy of me*; anyone who loves his son or daughter *more* than me *is not worthy of me*; and anyone who does *not* take his cross and follow me *is not worthy of me*." (Matthew 10:34-38)

"*Blessed* are you when men *hate* you, when they *exclude* you and *insult* you and *reject* your name as evil, *because of the Son of Man.*" (Luke 6:22)

"If anyone comes to me and does *not* hate his father and mother, his wife and children, his brothers and sisters--yes, even his own life-- *he cannot be my disciple*. And anyone who does *not* carry his cross and follow me *cannot be my disciple*." (Luke 14:26-27)

"Am I now trying to win the approval *of men, or of God*? Or am I trying to please men? *If I were still trying to please men, I would not be a servant of Christ*." (Galatians 1:10)

I can't tell you how amazing it is to take part in your first healing miracle! When you watch Jesus doing awesome healing miracles it will get you so excited that it won't matter what people say!

When people are experiencing pain and you lay hands on them, sometimes they will say, "I can still find a little bit of pain there." People have a tendency to focus on the 5% of pain that is still there and miss the fact that 95% of the pain was miraculously healed! Have them praise God for the miracle (and you praise Him too, of course) and both of you continue thanking Jesus for the remaining 5% of the pain to go as well.

Thanking Jesus over and over tends to bring about more healing. Always thank Jesus for the healing, even before anything happens.

It is very helpful to keep ourselves immersed in the Scriptures where Jesus gave us the authority to heal the sick, because this helps keep our faith at a high level. Periodically review the handouts in this Healing Book in order to keep this information fresh in your mind and keep studying the examples of healing in the Bible so that the Holy Spirit can reveal new things to you.

The Bible says that "the word of God is *living* and *active*" (Hebrews 4:12), but the Word of God needs to be living *in* you in order for it to be *active* in your life! (see Joshua 1:8, Proverbs 4:20-22, Psalms 1:1-3, and 119:10-20).

Continue to grow in spiritual maturity so that God will be able to trust you with more authority to use His power.

Walk in boldness and confidence in the Lord, because Christianity is not a religion, it is a *relationship* and a way of life that you live 24 hours a day. Never do anything half-heartedly for the Lord! (Colossians 3:23-24). Don't wait for

God to call you into a healing ministry, He has *already* called you! Don't let fear stop you. Don't limit God.

Speak with authority and say it like you mean it. Don't get discouraged, you'll get better with practice and experience and learning. Be "dead to self" like the apostle Paul said: "I have been crucified with Christ and I no longer live, but Christ lives in me" (Galatians 2:20).

Dead people don't care if they look foolish when someone doesn't get healed and dead people don't have any agendas of their own, so they are open to the leading of the Holy Spirit.

Above all, love those people out there! Get them healed and get them saved and give Jesus lots of opportunities to receive glory and praise and honor!

May the Lord richly bless your life with fruitfulness for the Kingdom as you go out and continue His evangelism and healing ministry and as you train others to do the same until He returns.

YOU can heal the sick in Jesus' Name!

The Proof is in the Bible

There is a guide given to us in God's Word. The Word cannot turn back void. The purpose of this Book is to give you some ideas of what to do and say in order to cast out demons and to demonstrate awesome healing miracles for the glory of the Lord.

I'm not trying to prove that I have any kind of special ability to heal people (I don't have any special ability, its all Jesus). What I'm trying to impart to you is that if you are a Christian then *you* can heal the sick in Jesus' Name!

You don't need any proof from me because you have plenty of proof from the Bible (as I try to demonstrate in this Book) and because when you step out in faith and begin laying hands on the sick then you will probably see plenty of healing miracles with your own eyes.

You can document all of your own proof that you want! I have no desire to convince you that *I* have seen miracles, I want *you* to see miracles!

They have found that the more specific we are when we command healing, the more likely it is that the person will be healed. Consider that Jesus was full of faith and He could say to a person, "Be healed."

However, we are human and fallible and we usually only have *small* faith, so healing is sometimes more effective when our limited faith is "targeted" more specifically.

How to Lay Hands on the Sick

This Chapter is to get you back to the basic principle of laying hands on the sick. When you do some of the things in this Book, I believe that you will begin seeing some amazing miracles of healing right in front of your eyes! I am not saying that everyone you lay hands on will be healed and not everyone who is healed will be healed instantly, but as you continue to be faithful you will see God confirming His Word as awesome healings begin taking place for the glory of the Lord.

In this section I am going to describe several healing techniques that have been developed over the years.

It is important for us to listen to the Holy Spirit when ministering to people, but it's not guaranteed that we'll always be able to hear from Him. So what do we do if someone needs to be healed but we're not hearing anything specific from the Holy Spirit? The apostle Paul said to imitate him as he imitates the Lord and other New Testament authors said essentially the same thing (1 Corinthians 4:16, 1 Thessalonians 1:6, Hebrews 6:12, 13:7, 3 John 1:11), which means that it is perfectly Scriptural to imitate fruitful Christians as role models. Therefore, if the Holy Spirit is not telling us anything specific when we lay hands on someone and we're not sure what to do, we can try saying or doing something that someone else said or did when there was a divine healing. That is the main reason for describing the techniques that other people use when successfully ministering healing.

These techniques are not meant to be treated as "rituals" and they are not necessary for divine healings to occur. However, it turns out to be quite helpful to be able to watch a person's arm growing out (for example) in order to see that the miracle is taking place and in order to see when the healing is finished. If other people are able to witness the miracle then it blesses them and increases their faith and God gets the extra glory and praise from those witnesses. Not to mention the testimonies of those witnesses as they excitedly share the story with family and friends. So it is good when other people can witness the miracle (unless the Holy Spirit tells you to do the healing privately) and there is nothing unscriptural about people witnessing miraculous healings since that happened repeatedly throughout the Gospels and Acts.

However, the glory must all go to God and it must never be a prideful thing on the part of the person doing the laying-on of hands.

Bear in mind that different Christians minister healing in different ways and that there is no "formula" for healing in the Bible. The following techniques are simply some of the ways that the Hunters minister healing and many other people (myself included) have seen amazing miracles by using these techniques. Other Christians teach different things about how to heal the sick and they see miraculous healings as well. It is important to listen to the Holy Spirit, but if we're not hearing anything specific then sometimes we can see miracles simply by imitating what others have done.

So here are some things that you can do and say when a person needs to be healed: "Growing Out Arms & Legs"

When people have upper back or shoulder problems, one arm often appears to be shorter than the other arm because some muscles or bones are damaged or are out of alignment, causing the pain. When God heals the back or shoulder, you can visibly watch the shorter arm grow out until it is the same length as the other arm. Statistics show that as much as 80% of the population has had some kind of back pain or injury, so this technique will come in handy fairly often.

Have the person stand up straight with his toes pointing forward and make sure his toes are lined up with each other (so his body isn't slightly twisted).

Then have him stretch his arms and fingers out in front of him as far as they will go. Have him hold his fingers out straight, with his palms facing each other. Have him put his palms together, then he can bend his elbows and look at his fingertips while his palms are pressed together so that he can see whether or not his arms are the same length. Now have him stretch his arms and fingers out in front again, palms facing each other but not quite touching. The purpose of having him stretch his arms out like this is so that you can visibly see the miracle taking place as the shorter arm grows out and also so that you will know when Jesus is finished doing the healing.

Now put your hands under his hands so that his hands are resting on the palms of your hands.

The power of the Holy Spirit will flow through your hands into his arms in order to heal him (you might not feel the power flow through you, but I sometimes find that my hand or the other person's hand has gotten fairly hot). You might mention that his arms will probably get a little tired, but that's a small price to pay for being healed.

To command the healing, say something along these lines (just say it quietly but with authority and expectation and remember to keep watching his fingertips): "In Jesus' Name I take authority and dominion over this back and shoulder area. I command the neck and back to be healed and I command the shoulders to be even and everything to go back into place, in Jesus' Name.

I command the muscles, nerves, ligaments and tendons to be healed and to go back to their normal position and normal length and strength, in Jesus' Name. I rebuke all pain and command it to go, all stiffness go, all immobility be removed, in Jesus' Name. I command the vertebrae and discs and shoulders to line up perfectly and everything to be healed in Jesus' Name. Thank You, Jesus!"

Sometimes the shorter arm will grow out before you finish saying this. If not, tell the person to thank Jesus and just keep thanking Him and giving praise and glory to God while commanding the arm to grow out. As the arm grows out, keep watching the fingertips because I usually see the shorter arm continue to grow until it is *longer* than the other arm, then it reverses itself and gets shorter until both arms are the same length.

Does it sound strange to *command* a healing in this way? Notice that you are not commanding Jesus or the Holy Spirit to do anything; you are simply obeying Scripture when you command a healing. To show you what I mean, let's first take a look at a couple of examples of the word "rebuke" to see that a rebuke is a command or an order. Notice what Jesus said when He rebuked Peter: "But when Jesus turned and looked at his disciples, he *rebuked* Peter. *"Get behind me*, Satan!" he said." (Mark 8:33)

How did Jesus rebuke Peter? He issued a command: "Get behind me, Satan!" A rebuke is a command or an order (Jesus was actually rebuking the devil who had put a thought into Peter's mind).

Many times Jesus rebuked evil spirits and (Mark 9:25) gives us an example of how He rebuked them: "When Jesus saw that a crowd was running to the scene, he *rebuked* the evil spirit. "You deaf and mute spirit," he said, "*I command you, come out of him and never enter him again*." (Mark 9:25)

How did Jesus rebuke the demon? He issued a command: "*I command you, come out of him and never enter him again.*" To rebuke something or someone is to issue an order or a command and the same Greek word is used in both of these examples of the word "rebuke."

Now that we know what the word "rebuke" means, here's the point I want to make. This same Greek word for "rebuke" is used when describing how Jesus healed a woman's fever: "So he bent over her and *rebuked the fever, and it left her. She got up at once and began to wait on them.*" (Luke 4:39)

To rebuke something is to issue an order or a command. Jesus laid hands on the woman (Matthew 8:15) and *commanded* the fever to go and it did. Jesus *spoke to* the fever and commanded it to be gone and this is what we need to do when we lay hands on people. Notice that Jesus dealt with the fever in exactly the same way that He dealt with the demon in (Mark 9:25 above). Jesus saw sickness as an *enemy*, and so should we!

You might be thinking at this point, "*But Jesus is the Son of God, of course He could command healing to take place. That doesn't mean that we have the right to do what He did!*" Ah, but Jesus *gave* us the right and the responsibility to do what He did!

"Believe me when I say that I am in the Father and the Father is in me; or at least believe on the evidence of the *miracles* themselves. I tell you the truth, *anyone who has faith in me will do what I have been doing*. He will do *even greater things than these*, because I am going to the Father. And I will do whatever you ask in my name, so that the Son may bring glory to the Father. You may ask me for anything in my name, and I will do it. *If you love me, you will obey what I command.*" (John 14:11-15)

Jesus said that *anyone* who has faith in Him will do the miraculous things He did! If you are a Christian then He is talking about you, so substitute your name into this passage and then read it again. Here's how this passage looks with my name: "at least believe on the evidence of the *miracles* themselves. I tell you the truth, *Bill will do what I have been doing*. Bill will do even greater things than these, because I am going to the Father. ... *If Bill loves me, Bill will obey what I command*." (John 14:11-15)

Try reading it with *your* name! Jesus said that believers will do the *same* miraculous things that He did and He said that if we love Him then we will *obey* Him. If we refuse to believe what He said then aren't we calling Jesus a liar?

In fact, Jesus specifically told us that we can *command* things and expect them to happen, *if* we have faith: "Seeing a fig tree by the road, he went up to it but found nothing on it except leaves. Then *he said to it*, "May you never bear fruit again!" *Immediately the tree withered*. When the disciples saw this, they were amazed. "How did the fig tree wither so quickly?" they asked. Jesus replied, "I tell you the truth, *if you have faith and do not doubt*, not only can *you* do what was done to the fig tree, but also *you can say to this mountain*, 'Go, throw yourself into the sea,' and it *will* be done. *If you believe, you will receive whatever you ask for in prayer*." (Matthew 21:19-22)

Jesus spoke a command to the fig tree and immediately it withered. Then He told the disciples that *they* could do the same thing! In fact, He went on to say that *they* could command a mountain to throw itself into the sea and it would be done! In the Great Commission, Jesus commanded the disciples to continue making *new* disciples, teaching us new disciples to obey all of these things as well (Matthew 28:18-20). Was Jesus saying that we should go out and re-arrange mountain ranges and make all fig trees become withered and dead? No, Jesus was giving us *principles* to teach us how faith works.

After saying that we can command a mountain to throw itself into the sea, Jesus said in the passage above that we *will* receive whatever we ask for in prayer, *if we believe*.

In other words, after we command the mountain, when it is removed then we have received what we asked for in prayer.

On another occasion Jesus said: "I tell you the truth, *if you have faith* as small as a mustard seed, *you can say to this mountain*, 'Move from here to there' and it *will* move. *Nothing will be impossible for you*." (Matthew 17:20)

Notice that Jesus did not say "nothing will be impossible for *God*." He said that nothing will be impossible for *you* when you speak to your mountains in faith.

Try substituting your name into this passage just like we did a moment ago. Here's how it looks with my name: "I tell you the truth, *if Bill has faith* as small as a mustard seed, *Bill can say to this mountain*, 'Move from here to there' and it *will* move. *Nothing will be impossible for Bill*." (Matthew 17:20)

Try reading it with *your* name!

Do you see what Jesus was saying? Jesus said over and over that we are to *speak to* the mountains in our lives and *command* them, believing that what we command will be done. This is exactly what Jesus did when He rebuked the woman's fever in (Luke 4:39).

Jesus was teaching us a principle about faith and when we apply this principle to healing we can see that the "mountain" which we are speaking to is for the sickness or disease or injury to go and the body to be healed. This is exactly what Jesus did when He commanded demons to come out, when He commanded the woman's fever to go, when He commanded people's bodies to be healed and so on.

Jesus apparently wanted to be sure that we would really grab hold of His message because He said it again on yet another occasion: He replied, "*If you have faith* as small as a mustard seed, *you can say to this mulberry tree*, 'Be uprooted and planted in the sea,' and *it will obey you*." (Luke 17:6)

If we have faith, we can *speak to* a mulberry tree and *command* it to jump into the sea and it *will* obey us! Furthermore, Jesus said that *everything* is possible for us if we will just believe: "If you can?" said Jesus. "*Everything is possible for him who believes*." (Mark 9:23)

Jesus did not say that everything is possible for *God*, He said that everything is possible for *you* if you will believe! Try substituting your name into this passage just like we did in the passages above. Here's how it looks with my name: "*Everything is possible for Bill*." (Mark 9:23)

Try reading it with *your* name!

In the Great Commission, Jesus specifically said that we can believe for divine protection as we carry out our commission and He specifically told us what all believers are to do: "And these signs will accompany *those who believe*: In my name they will *drive out demons*; they will *speak in new tongues*; they will pick up snakes with their hands; and when they drink deadly poison, it will not hurt them at all; *they will place their hands on sick people, and they will get well*." (Mark 16:17-18)

If you are a believer then Jesus has commissioned you, in writing, to do some things which are part of your "job responsibilities" (so to speak) as a member of His body, the Church. What did He command you to do in the passage above?

In addition to sharing the Good News, you have been called to cast out demons, speak in tongues and lay hands on the sick! Here is how this passage looks with my name: "And these signs will accompany *Bill*: In my name *Bill will drive out demons*; *Bill will speak in new tongues*; Bill will have divine protection available to him *Bill will place his hands on sick people, and they will get well*." (Mark 16:17-18)

Try reading it with *your* name!

Now let's summarize the things that Jesus said in the above passages. The Bible is inspired, infallible Scripture which was written to *teach* you and me, so let's personalize all of these messages so that we can really grasp what Jesus is trying to get across to us.

Jesus cannot lie and here is what He says about me: If Bill has faith, Bill can do the *same* things that Jesus did (John 14:12).
If Bill has faith, Bill can do *greater* things than Jesus did (John 14:12).

If Bill has faith and does not doubt, Bill can *command* a fig tree to wither, and it *will* be done (Matthew 21:19-22).
If Bill has faith and does not doubt, Bill can *command* a mountain to throw itself into the sea, and it *will* be done (Matthew 21:19-22).

If Bill believes, Bill *will* receive whatever Bill asks for in prayer, such as commanding a mountain to jump into the sea (Matthew 21:19-22).

If Bill has faith, Bill can *command* a mountain to move from here to there, and it *will* be done. (Matthew 17:20)

If Bill has faith, *nothing* will be impossible for Bill (Matthew 17:20).

If Bill has faith, Bill can *command* a mulberry tree to be uprooted and plant itself in the sea, and it *will* be done (Luke 17:6).

If Bill believes, *everything* is possible for Bill (Mark 9:23).

If Bill believes, Bill will *cast out* demons, Bill will speak in *tongues*, and Bill will *lay hands on the sick* and see miraculous healings. (Mark 16:15-18)

Try reading these things with *your* name, because Jesus says the same things about you!

You have probably seen some of these passages before, but do you believe them? Every one of these promises is true, if we will simply *believe* them! Jesus made all of these promises and if we choose not to believe that they are true then aren't we calling Jesus a liar?

This is why we are supposed to *command* the healing instead of praying and asking God to do it and this is why there is not a single example anywhere in the Gospels or Acts of Jesus or the apostles asking God to heal a sick person.

Now, let's say that the person was injured and had three crushed vertebrae or discs, for example and had surgery for it.

You should then add something like this while you are commanding the healing: "In the Name of Jesus I command a creative miracle. I command the vertebrae and discs to be made new, three brand new ones in Jesus' Name. I command all scar tissue to go, all scar tissue dissolve, in Jesus' Name."

Recall that God did a creative miracle when He created Adam (in other words, God created something new). God is still fully capable of doing creative healing miracles today, such as replacing damaged vertebrae. He hasn't lost His touch! It is no more difficult for God to put in a *new* part than it is for Him to heal an old part, but this doesn't usually happen spontaneously. God has put it into our hands to request it ("You do not have, *because you do not ask God*" - James 4:2).

This illustrates why it is important to ask the person some questions about his sickness or injury. You need to tailor what you say in order to address their specific needs.

Once arms are the same length, have him bend and stretch his back while thanking Jesus. This is putting his faith into action and it will also help determine whether the healing is complete and all pain is gone. Always give God the glory for every bit of improvement! Don't worry if you have to lay hands on the person a second time (or more) to complete the healing, even Jesus sometimes did that.

"He took the blind man by the hand and led him outside the village. When he had spit on the man's eyes and put his hands on him, Jesus asked, "Do you see anything?" He looked up and said, "I see people; they look like trees walking around." *Once more Jesus put his hands on the man's eyes.* Then his eyes were opened, his sight was restored, and he saw everything clearly." (Mark 8:23-25)

Using this Technique

I've seen many healed of back, neck and many other alignment problems. God can be our chiropractor. The top 7 vertebrae (the "neck bones") are called the cervical vertebrae. The next 12 are called the dorsal (or thoracic) vertebrae. The last 5 are called the lumbar vertebrae. Hundreds of thousands of nerve fibers from the brain pass through little openings in these vertebrae to control all the various parts and organs of the body. Slight dislocations of the vertebrae can pinch these nerves and interfere with the nerve impulses being passed to and from the brain.

"Growing out arms" can be used to heal problems caused by pinched nerves running through the dorsal vertebrae to the heart, lungs, gall bladder, stomach, liver, kidneys, and intestines. These problems include bronchial conditions, throat conditions, arm and shoulder pain or numbness, bursitis, asthma, coughs, thyroid conditions, chest pains, congestion, palpitation, "nervous" or fast or irregular heart, pleurisy, jaundice, shingles, stomach upsets, heartburn, fever, low blood pressure, poor circulation, ulcers, hives and so on.

To heal one of these problems, grow out the person's arms while commanding the condition to be healed, even if the person does not appear to have one arm shorter than the other. Commanding everything to come in alignment and be healed.

Now, can God heal people even if we don't use techniques such as this? Sure He can! The purpose of ministering healing in this way is simply so that you can see when the Lord is finished doing the healing. Plus, it is exciting to watch the Lord shifting people's muscles and bones right in front of your eyes!

"Growing Out Legs"

When people have lower back pain, sometimes one leg appears to be shorter than the other.

Have the person sit in a chair, pressed all the way back against the back of the chair (to ensure that he's not twisted slightly in the chair).

Have him stick his legs straight out, then grab hold of his legs at his ankles (with your thumbs to the inside of his legs and your fingers to the outside), then put your thumbs on the highest point of his ankle bones (i.e. on the "peak" of his ankles). Now bring his legs together so that your thumbs are touching and you will easily be able to see if his legs are different lengths because your two thumbs won't line up with each other. Say: "In the Name of Jesus I take authority and dominion over this lower back and pelvic area. I command all of the muscles in the pelvic area to be relaxed and the pelvis to be adjusted into proper alignment, in Jesus' Name. I command the muscles, nerves, ligaments and tendons to be healed and to go back to their normal position and normal length and strength, in Jesus' Name.

I rebuke all pain and command it to go, all stiffness go, all immobility be removed, in Jesus' Name. Thank You, Jesus!"

The purpose of this technique is so that you can watch the miracle as the leg grows out and so that you will know when Jesus is finished healing the person.

Again, if the person tells you that he has had some specific injury in this area then command healing to those parts and command a creative miracle if needed.

Problems that can be healed with this technique

"Growing out legs" can be used to heal problems caused by pinched nerves running through the lumbar vertebrae to the appendix, bowels, genitals, bladder and lower limbs. These problems include hiccups, lowered resistance, dyspepsia, circulatory problems, rheumatism, some types of sterility, impotence, "female problems," diarrhea, constipation, knee pain, varicose veins, prostate problems, bed wetting, backaches, cold feet, leg cramps, hemorrhoids, ankle swelling and so on.

Again, "when in doubt, grow it out." To heal one of these problems, grow out the person's legs while commanding the condition to be healed, even if the person does not appear to have one leg shorter than the other.

Carpal Tunnel Technique

This is a fantastic technique that works. If someone has carpal tunnel syndrome, have him touch the tip of his thumb to the tip of his pinky finger to form a circle. If you put your finger inside the circle, you will easily be able to pull your finger through his thumb and pinky because there is no strength there. After he is healed then he will be able to resist and you won't be able to pull through very easily.

When nerves travel through rigid tunnels (such as the ones in our wrists), if tissues swell up within the tunnel then they pinch the nerves, causing great pain. Therefore, hold the person's wrist and say: "In Jesus' Name I take authority and dominion over this wrist area. I command these tunnels to open up and all inflammation and swelling to be healed, in Jesus' Name. I command the muscles, nerves, ligaments and tendons to be healed and to go back to their proper length and strength, in Jesus' Name. Pain, I rebuke you, I command all pain to go now, in Jesus' Name. Thank You, Jesus."

Have the person touch the tip of his thumb to the tip of his pinky again. There should now be strong resistance when you try to pull your finger through his thumb and pinky.

There are other places where nerves run through small tunnels, such as the elbow ("tennis elbow") and the ankle ("tarsal tunnel syndrome") and these can also be healed with this type of command.

In a moment I will describe some specific commands that have been found helpful when healing various common diseases, but first we need to talk about... Casting Out Demons. This is my next Chapter you must read.

Casting Out Demons

Sometimes when dealing with the sick you may need to cast out demons. Let's say that a woman asks you to heal her back because her spine is bent over and she has not been able to straighten up in years. What would you do?

You could try laying hands on her back and commanding her spine to straighten. You could try growing out her arms and commanding the vertebrae and discs to be healed and to return to their proper position and alignment. Remember the handy expression, "when in doubt, grow it out."

However, there's another expression which will sometimes come in handy: "When in doubt, *cast* it out."

Many problems are caused by demons. When the demons are cast out or temporarily "shut down" then the affliction can often be healed. In this section I am going to describe something you can say to command afflicting spirits to leave, but this is not really meant to be a teaching on deliverance.

Deliverance is a full subject of its own which is beyond the scope of this article. Still, some demons seem to leave fairly quickly and easily, which will bring relief to the afflicted person.

Here is how Jesus healed a woman with a problem such as the one I described above: "On a Sabbath Jesus was teaching in one of the synagogues and *a woman was there who had been crippled by a spirit for eighteen years. She was bent over and could not straighten up at all.* When Jesus saw her, he called her forward and said to her, "Woman, you are set free from your infirmity." Then *he put his hands on her, and immediately she straightened up* and praised God." (Luke 13:10-13)

The woman was bent over because of an afflicting spirit. Jesus laid hands on her and the spirit left and when she put her faith into action by straightening up she was immediately healed.

Notice that Jesus called demons by the things they did: When Jesus saw that a crowd was running to the scene, he *rebuked* the evil spirit. "*You deaf and mute spirit*," he said, "*I command you, come out of him and never enter him again.*" (Mark 9:25)

Jesus addressed this demon by what it did: "You deaf and mute spirit."

Scripture also speaks of lying spirits (1 Kings 22:22), a spirit of dizziness (Isaiah 19:14), a spirit of prostitution (Hosea 5:4), a spirit that makes people slaves to fear (Romans 8:15), a spirit of stupor (Romans 11:8), a spirit of timidity (2 Timothy 1:7), a spirit of falsehood (1 John 4:6), and so on.

When casting out demons, we call them by what they do and we can often cast them out just as Jesus did in (Mark 9:25) above.

In (Matthew 12:29), Jesus spoke of binding the strongman before robbing his house, so before we rob the devil of his hold on people, we first bind him as I'll demonstrate in a moment.

One of the most important things when dealing with demons is to *know* who you are in Christ. Remember that anytime the devil tries to afflict us, before the battle even begins the outcome has *already* been declared: *WE WIN!* Jesus has disarmed the powers and principalities of darkness and therefore we have nothing to fear from them: "And having *disarmed* the powers and authorities, he made a *public spectacle* of them, *triumphing over them* by the cross." (Colossians 2:15)

When a police officer or an FBI agent shows people his badge of authority, he usually gets immediate respect and people will immediately do what he says. Jesus has given us *His* badge of authority over *all* the power of the enemy: "I have given you *authority* to trample on snakes and scorpions and to overcome *all* the power of the enemy" (Luke 10:19)

We overcome the enemy because Jesus lives in us: "This is the spirit of the antichrist, which you have heard is coming and even now is already in the world. You, dear children, are from God and *have overcome them, because the one who is in you is greater than the one who is in the world.*" (1 John 4:3-4)

So you see, we have nothing to fear from the devil or his demons when we *know* who we are in Christ and we *know* the authority that He has given us over *all* the power of the enemy. Smith Wigglesworth, who was a powerful man of prayer and a powerful man of God, was once awakened in the middle of the night by an overwhelming presence of evil in his bedroom and he saw what appeared to be the devil standing there at the foot of his bed. What would you or I do in such a situation? Smith Wigglesworth simply said, "Oh, it's only you," and then he rolled over and went back to sleep! He knew his authority in Christ and therefore he knew he had nothing to fear. Neither do we, praise the Lord! Even if demons attach themselves to our lives in some way, we have the authority to break their attachments and command them to leave us.

Notice in the (Mark 9:25) passage (above) that when Jesus cast the spirit out of the woman there were no shrieks or manifestations, the woman was simply healed. This is often how it will be when you cast out spirits as well. For example, certain diseases such as bursitis are often caused by demons and when you command the spirit to leave, the person will discover that his pain is gone, even though there was no direct evidence of demonic involvement. Sometimes a demon will come into manifestation and scream at you and try to shock or frighten you, but don't be afraid of it and don't "chat" with it, just command it to leave and never return. They are all liars, so don't listen to anything they say. If they come into manifestation and say things or do things, command them sternly to be quiet and to come out in Jesus' Name (Mark 1:25).

Keep in mind what the apostle Paul said: "*Hate what is evil*; cling to what is good" (Romans 12:9).

However, we also need to recognize that some people have become severely demonized, whether through involvement in the occult or from being victims of child abuse or other forms of abuse, or for other reasons. They may require more experienced Christian deliverance counseling in order to be set free.

When casting demons out of children, we don't want to upset or frighten the children because they are probably already frightened as it is. Don't shout and scream at the demon, don't yell at it in tongues (it won't be able to understand you!), simply smile soothingly and lovingly at the child to help keep him or her calm, then command the demon in a quiet voice to come out and stay out.

If you say it like you mean it then the demon will know it. Remember that speaking with authority does not mean shouting or screaming. A parent of a misbehaving child in a store can whisper, "Get over here *right now*!" and the child knows that the parent means business!

Diseases which are "incurable" according to medical science are often caused by demons. Doctors can't cure the disease because they don't understand the underlying cause of the disease, which is a spirit. When someone tells you they have an "incurable" disease, try binding the devil and then casting out the spirit of that disease (such as cancer): "Devil, I bind you by the power of the Spirit of God in the Name of Jesus and I cut off all your power. Now you foul spirit of cancer, I bind you, I break your authority and I cancel your assignment in the Name of Jesus.

I command you to come out now in the Name of Jesus and don't you ever return!"

As I said, this is not really meant to be a teaching on deliverance; this is simply a basic introduction to the subject. But since some demons leave a person fairly quickly and easily, sometimes we can cast them out with commands such as the one above. To learn more about how demons operate and to learn some powerful prayers for preventing demons from interfering with a healing, I highly recommend a book called Defeating the Demonic Realm.

Diseases and Afflictions

After years of experience with healings and miracles, God has given me some powerful insight that works. This list gives you some examples of how various diseases have been successfully healed and you can use the same basic concepts to guide you in what to say concerning other diseases that you will come across.

These are principles that other ministries have used effectively in their healing ministry and which other people (myself included) have found to be effective at times as well. However, healing the sick is not an exact science and there are many people in the healing ministry who teach on divine healing in different ways.

It is always important to pray for the Holy Spirit's guidance and to do whatever He tells you to do. But if you are not hearing anything specific from the Holy Spirit then try using commands such as these:

Addictions

Make sure that the person wants to be free of his addiction and lead him through a "sinner's prayer" if he is not already saved.

Addiction:

"Devil I bind you by the power of the Spirit of God in the Name of Jesus and I cut off all your power. Now you foul spirit of alcohol addiction, I cancel your assignment in the Name of Jesus. I command you to come out now in the Name of Jesus and don't you ever return!"

Command the person's body to be healed and the desire for the alcohol (or drugs or tobacco or whatever) to be gone in Jesus' Name.

AIDS/HIV

If the disease was contracted through any form of sinful activity (homosexuality, promiscuous sexual activity, sharing needles for illegal drugs, etc.), then these things need to be renounced and repented of. Make sure that the person is saved and take him or her through the plan of salvation if necessary.

Then rebuke the infection and take authority over it in Jesus' Name, and cast out the spirit of AIDS in Jesus' Name. Command the entire immune system to be healed and restored in Jesus' Name. Command the entire body to be healed and restored to normal in Jesus' Name.

Allergies and Asthma

Allergies are the body's bad reaction to foreign substances and they sometimes run in families. Asthma, a lung condition causing wheezing and shortness of breath, also can run in families and is often associated with allergies.

Cast out the spirit of inheritance and the spirit of allergy or asthma, then lay hands on the person's head and command the immune system to return to normal and all the tissues and organs to be healed and to function normally, in the Name of Jesus. "Grow out" the person's arms and legs, commanding any pinched nerves to be released in the Name of Jesus.

For asthma, also speak the peace of God into the person's life.

Alzheimer's Disease

A disease with an unknown origin which results in the deterioration of the brain, resulting in loss of memory and reasoning abilities.

Cast out the spirits of inheritance and Alzheimer's disease. Charles and Frances also say to speak a creative miracle, commanding a new brain. Remember, it is just as easy for God to put in a new part as it is for Him to heal an original part. After you make these commands to the person's body, leave the results up to God.

I have been told that Alzheimer's Disease might be caused by some type of build-up on the cells in the memory area of the brain, which disrupts the electrical impulses between the cells. Apparently the symptoms of Alzheimer's Disease were reduced (or were completely gone) after a surgical procedure to remove this build-up!

Anything that doctors can do, God can do, so you might try commanding all of the "junk" which has built-up on the cells in the brain to completely be removed.

Amyotrophic Lateral Sclerosis
(ALS, also called Lou Gehrig's Disease)

ALS causes an irreversible degeneration of the nerves in the spinal cord, causing progressive weakness.

Cast out the spirit of ALS. "Grow out" the person's arms and legs, commanding new nerves in the body and the spinal cord.

Aneurysm

This is a condition where the wall of an artery has become thin and stretched out and is in danger of rupturing.

Lay hands on the area and command a creative miracle, new arteries with strong healthy walls, in the Name of Jesus. Command normal blood flow to be restored in the Name of Jesus.

Arthritis

Arthritis is a painful inflammation of the joints. It has been found to be caused by a spirit and/or by anger or resentment or unforgiveness, which causes an overabundance of adrenaline to be released into the body. The body can't absorb this excess adrenaline so it goes into the kidneys, which are unable to carry off this excess. Finally it settles in the joints, causing painful swelling.

Have the person release any anger or resentment by forgiving the people involved. Then bind and cast out the spirit of arthritis in the Name of Jesus. "Grow out" the person's arms and legs, commanding the swelling to be healed and all pain to go in the Name of Jesus.

Astigmatism
An abnormally-shaped eye.

Lay hands on the person's eyes, commanding all parts of the eyes to be healed and to return to normal shape, in Jesus' Name.

Blindness

Try to determine the cause of the blindness (glaucoma, cataracts, infection, injury, etc.) and address it specifically, if possible. Also try to determine the extent of the blindness so that you will be able to tell how much improvement there has been.

Bind and cast out the spirit of blindness in Jesus' Name. Lay hands on the person's eyes, commanding healing to the eyes and commanding perfect eyesight to be restored in Jesus' Name. Command a creative miracle to the nerves, eye structures and brain as needed, in Jesus' Name. After each step, check to see if the blindness has been healed, but be sensitive to the fact that normal light will probably seem abnormally bright to a person who has been blind.

Blood Pressure Problems

Ask if the doctor has diagnosed anything which may be causing the problems such as (diabetes, arteriosclerosis, kidney problems, heart disease, etc.), then make specific commands against these problems, in the Name of Jesus.

Command the heart to be healed and command the vessels and arteries to be opened and to function properly with normal elasticity, in the Name of Jesus. "Grow out" the person's arms and legs, commanding the muscles and nerves to be normal and to allow blood to flow properly, in the Name of Jesus.

Bronchitis

Bronchitis is an irritation and inflammation of the bronchial tubes, connecting the nose to the lungs.

Rebuke the infection in the Name of Jesus (similar to what Jesus did in Luke 4:39), then lay hands on the upper chest and throat, commanding the tissues in the bronchial tubes and lungs to be healed and to function normally, in the Name of Jesus.

Bunions

Swelling in the main joint of the big toe.

Cast out the spirit of inheritance and rebuke the inflammation, in Jesus' Name. "Grow out" the person's legs, commanding the toe and bones to go back into place, the ligaments to strengthen and the foot to be normal, in Jesus' Name.

Bursitis

Bursitis is an inflammation of the sacs of fluid which help tendons and muscles move across bones.

Cast out the spirit of bursitis in the Name of Jesus, then lay hands on the area and command all pain and inflammation to go in the Name of Jesus. Command all tissues to be healed and normal fluid to be produced for painless movement of the joints, in the Name of Jesus.

Cancer

This includes any malignant tumors, leukemia, lymphoma and so on.

Bind and cast out the spirit of cancer. Lay hands on the person and curse the seed, the root and the cells of the cancer, commanding every cancer cell in the body to die (similar principle to Jesus' example of the fig tree that He cursed in Mark 11:21). Command the bone marrow to produce pure healthy blood and command healing and restoration to all organs and tissues affected by the cancer. Command the body's defensive "killer cells" to multiply and attack and kill all of the cancer cells. All of these commands are given in the Name of Jesus, of course.

Cataracts

Clouding of the lens of the eye caused by layers of the eye drying out. Not cancerous.

Lay hands on the eyes and cast out the spirit of inheritance, in Jesus' Name. Command blood and fluid to flow through the "onion" layers of the eyes, restoring perfect vision, in Jesus' Name.

Colds and Flu

"Grow out" the person's arms and legs, rebuking the infection and commanding the blood vessels to open to allow blood to flow freely, ridding the affected areas of germs, in Jesus' Name. Command the intestinal symptoms to go and command the body to accept and utilize food properly, in Jesus' Name. Suggest that the person drink 8 glasses of water a day to flush out the germs.

Crohn's Disease

Inflammation of the mucous membranes in the intestinal tract.

Cast out the spirit of Crohn's Disease and rebuke the infection. "Grow out" the person's arms and legs, commanding the tissues of the bowels to be healed and to function normally.

Deafness

Deafness can be caused by an inherited spirit, a deaf spirit which has attached itself to the body, nerve failure (including pinched nerves), damaged eardrum and so on. Try to determine the cause of the deafness (if there has been a medical diagnosis) and determine the amount of hearing loss so that you are able to tell when there has been an improvement.

Cast out the spirits of deafness and inheritance. Gently put your fingers in the person's ears and command the deafness to go and normal hearing to be restored. "Grow out" the person's arms and legs, commanding any pinched nerves to be released and blood flow into the ears to be normal and commanding the hair-like nerves in the inner ear to grow. Command healing to the eardrum and command a brand new eardrum and bone structures, if needed. Lay hands on the sides of the head, commanding the temporal bones to rotate back into proper position. Everything is done in the Name of Jesus. After each step, check to see if the deafness has been healed, but be sensitive to the fact that normal sounds will probably seem abnormally loud to a person who has been deaf.

Diabetes

Improper insulin production in the pancreas.

In Jesus' Name, cast out the spirits of diabetes and inheritance. Command a new pancreas into the body and command any parts which were damaged by excess sugar to be healed and made whole, in Jesus' Name.

Down's Syndrome

A condition in which a child is born with 47 chromosomes in each cell instead of the normal 46. This condition is often characterized by certain facial features and by mental or learning challenges.

Bind and cast out the spirit of mongolism, in Jesus' Name. Charles and Frances also say to lay hands on the person's head, commanding a creative miracle, a new brain, in Jesus' Name.

Remember, it is just as easy for God to put in a new part as it is for Him to heal an original part. After you make these commands to the person's body, leave the results up to God. Command the person's cells to revert to the correct number of chromosomes and command the extra chromosome to go in Jesus' Name. Command the body to be healed and to function normally and command the facial features to be normal in Jesus' Name.

Eczema

Inflammation of the skin characterized by redness, flaking, or blistering.

Bind and cast out the spirit of eczema, then curse the eczema and command the inflammation to go in Jesus' Name.

Command the cells which manufacture skin to replace all of the damaged tissues and command the skin to return to normal function, texture and structure, in Jesus' Name.

Farsightedness
Nearsightedness

Farsightedness is the inability to see things up close. Nearsightedness is the inability to see things far off (also called Myopia).

Lay one hand over the eyes and place the other hand at the back of the head. Command the optic nerve to be healed and adjusted properly and command the lenses, nerves, ligaments and muscles to be adjusted to the proper length and strength and to work properly, in Jesus' Name.

Command the blood vessels in and around the eyes to be normal and command the circulation to be normal, in Jesus' Name. Command the muscles around the eyes to be relaxed and the eyeballs to return to the perfect form that they need for perfect vision, in Jesus' Name. Command the pressure in the eyes and the fluid in the eyes to be normal and command a creative miracle, restoring 20/20 vision, in Jesus' Name.

"Female Problems" or "Male Problems"

This refers to any problems with the reproductive system.

"Grow out" the person's legs, commanding all of the tissues, nerves and vessels to function normally and the sacrum (a bone which is down by the tailbone) to rotate into the correct position, in Jesus' Name. Command any infection or irritation to go and command all scar tissue to dissolve and all damaged parts to be restored and to function properly, in Jesus' Name. Command all hormones to be released within the body in normal amounts and command a divine diuretic to rid the body of any excess fluid, in Jesus' Name. Command the blood vessels to be normal and command the circulation to be normal, in Jesus' Name.

Glaucoma

Increased pressure within the eyeball.

Command the spirit of inheritance to come out in Jesus' Name. Command the canals of the eyes to open, allowing fluid to flow normally and the pressure to become normal, in Jesus' Name. Command any diseases or scar tissue to be healed and the eyes to return to normal, in Jesus' Name.

Ganglion Cyst

Hard fluid-filled lump, usually on the wrist.

Lay hands on the cyst, commanding it to dissolve and the fluid to be re-absorbed into the body, in Jesus' Name. Command the wrist structures, bones, muscles and tendons to go back into normal position in Jesus' Name. Command the joint lining to produce proper joint fluid, command the blood supply to be normal and command all pressure on the nerves to go back to normal and all pain to go, in Jesus' Name.

Headache

Lay hands on the person's head, commanding the blood to flow normally and all spasms of the vessels to release in Jesus' Name. If it's a migraine, cast out the spirit of migraine in Jesus' Name. Command a separation between the nerves and blood vessels where the pain is occurring, in Jesus' Name.

High Blood Pressure (also called Hypertension)

Command the entire blood system to be cleaned out and command the blood pressure to return to normal and remain there, in Jesus' Name. Suggest that the person spend time in the Word of God, relaxing with the Lord and eliminating any tension, stress, or fear.

Multiple Sclerosis

Bind and cast out the spirit of Multiple Sclerosis, in Jesus' Name. "Grow out" the person's arms and legs, commanding the nerves to be healed and to be restored to normal structure and function, in Jesus' Name. Command all parts of the body which have been affected by this disease to be healed and to function normally, in Jesus' Name.

Raising someone from the Dead It is just as easy for God to raise a person from the dead as it is for Him to heal anything else.

I showed that we have been commissioned to continue Jesus' earthly ministry until He returns at the end of the age and that His ministry consisted of preaching the Good News, healing the sick and casting out demons.

When John the Baptist sent two of his disciples to verify that Jesus was the Messiah, notice how Jesus validated His ministry: When John heard in prison what Christ was doing, he sent his disciples to ask him, "Are you the one who was to come, or should we expect someone else?" Jesus replied, "Go back and *report to John what you hear and see*: The blind receive sight, the lame walk, those who have leprosy are cured, the deaf hear, *the dead are raised*, and the good news is preached to the poor." (Matthew 11:2-5)

Raising the dead was part of Jesus' earthly ministry, which means it is something that we have the privilege of doing as we continue His ministry until He returns.

When Jesus sent the Twelve out to participate in His ministry for the first time, raising the dead was part of His commission to them: "Heal the sick, *raise the dead*, cleanse those who have leprosy, drive out demons. Freely you have received, freely give." (Matthew 10:8)

After Pentecost, the disciples went out to fulfill the Great Commission, continuing Jesus' earthly ministry. Not only did they preach the Good News, heal the sick and cast out demons as Jesus had done, they also raised the dead as Jesus had done: "Peter went with them and when he arrived he was taken upstairs to the room. All the widows stood around him, crying and showing him the robes and other clothing that Dorcas had made while she was still with them. *Peter sent them all out of the room*; then he got down on his knees and prayed.

Turning toward the *dead woman*, he said, "*Tabitha, get up*." She opened her eyes, and seeing Peter she sat up." (Acts 9:39-40)

"Seated in a window was a young man named Eutychus, who was sinking into a deep sleep as Paul talked on and on. When he was sound asleep, he fell to the ground from the third story and was *picked up dead.* Paul went down, *threw himself on the young man and put his arms around him.* "Don't be alarmed," he said. "*He's alive!*" (Acts 20:9-10)

As we go out and fulfill the Great Commission, continuing Jesus' earthly ministry until He returns, we have Scriptural authority for trying to raise the dead.

We can see in the examples above that the apostles raised the dead exactly like they did any other healing, by laying hands (or their whole body) on the person and commanding the person to get up.

This is exactly how Jesus raised the dead as well: "He went in and said to them, "Why all this commotion and wailing? The child is not *dead* but asleep." But they laughed at him. *After he put them all out*, he took the child's father and mother and the disciples who were with him, and went in where the child was. *He took her by the hand* and said to her, "Talitha cumi!" (which means, "*Little girl, I say to you, get up!*"). Immediately the girl stood up and walked around (she was twelve years old). At this they were completely astonished." (Mark 5:39-42)

"Then he went up and *touched the coffin*, and those carrying it stood still. He said, "*Young man, I say to you, get up!*" The dead man sat up and began to talk, and Jesus gave him back to his mother." (Luke 7:14-15)

When he had said this, Jesus called in a loud voice, "*Lazarus, come out!*" The dead man came out, his hands and feet wrapped with strips of linen, and a cloth around his face. Jesus said to them, "Take off the grave clothes and let him go." (John 11:43-44)

Notice that raising the dead is done in the same manner as any other healing. In other words, you lay hands on or near the dead person and make a command in Jesus'

Name. Keep in mind, though, that several modern-day resurrections required a few hours of calling for life to return in Jesus' Name.

WARNING!!! When dealing with the spirit of death be sure you are being led by the Holy Spirit or it could backfire on you.

There is obviously no way to guarantee how long it will take in each specific situation, but experience has shown that persistence pays off (see Luke 11:5-8).

Also notice that since doubt and unbelief can hinder healing, Jesus and the apostles sometimes made everyone leave the room before raising the dead.

When a person has some type of paralysis, it has been found very helpful to first cast out the spirit of death, because a paralyzed limb is essentially dead. Similarly, when a person is dead it has been found helpful to cast out the spirit of death and to command the spirit of life to return to the body. If the person committed suicide then there might be a spirit of suicide or a spirit of self-destruction hanging around, so cast them out as well. It is not normal for a person to desire to destroy himself, so suicide often stems from demonic oppression and therefore these types of spirits need to be cast out.

When a person dies, it is because the body has become damaged to the point where it cannot sustain life any longer. Therefore command the body to be healed as well as for life to return. For example, if the person has drowned, command the water in the lungs to disappear, command the lungs to be healed, command the brain to be healed or to be made new and so on. Use common sense based on the type of physical damage which brought about the death.

When a person dies, especially if it was a violent death, it can be difficult to have faith that he will live again. But remember, *everything* is easy for God!

Does the Bible say that we are to judge by the physical evidence whether or not God can do something? No, the Bible says we are to live by faith, *not* by sight. (2 Corinthians 5:7)

Don't let your faith be hindered by the physical evidence. Stand on the Word of God and on the commission which Jesus gave you in Scripture.

God is sovereign and it is up to Him to restore the person's life if He so chooses, but people do not often *spontaneously* return from the dead. Remember James' admonition: "You do not have, *because you do not ask God*" (James 4:2).

Be very sensitive to people's grief and emotions in their time of loss. Consider how devastating it can be if you build up their hope that their deceased loved one will be resurrected and then nothing happens. Also, how will people react if the deceased person suddenly comes back to life during the funeral or the viewing?

Pray hard for the Holy Spirit's guidance and be very sensitive to people's emotional states in their time of grief and loss.

Scoliosis

An abnormal curvature of the spine. Bind and cast out the spirit of scoliosis in Jesus' Name. "Grow out" the person's arms and legs, commanding the bones in the back and the ribs and other supporting structures to return to proper position and alignment, in Jesus' Name.

Remember, this list is simply intended to give you some ideas of how various afflictions have been successfully healed. This doesn't mean that you *have* to say these things. Sometimes people are healed when we simply repeat the Name "Jesus" over and over.

However, healing is often more successful when we are specific in what we command, so the above list is intended to give you some examples of how to be specific.

As I said earlier, these are commands that ministries (and others, such as myself) have used and which have been effective in ministering divine healing. Other Christians in the healing ministry have other teachings which have also been effective in ministering divine healing.

What If Someone Doesn't Get Healed?

This Chapter is for those times when people are not healed. I'll be the first to admit that although I have seen amazing miracles when I have laid hands on the sick, I have not had 100% success in ministering healing. I have never heard of anyone in modern times who has and there are several reasons for this.

For one thing, if we could be as full of faith and as sensitive to the Holy Spirit as Jesus was, then we would probably have the same degree of success in healing that Jesus did. But we're not, so we don't.

If you lay hands on someone and nothing seems to happen, there might be some issues that need to be dealt with such as fears doubts, theological misunderstandings about healing, demonic interference, emotional blockages and so on. These issues might require a number of sessions of prayer and teaching and the person might need to be referred to as a trained and experienced Christian counselor for counseling and/or deliverance.

I have sometimes found that half the pain was healed immediately when I laid hands on people and that more of the pain left when I laid hands on them a second time. The remaining pain was gone after a few minutes, or, in one recent case, overnight.

God does not usually do things according to a formula, so don't worry if a particular healing seems to be taking longer than other healings you have seen. Even Jesus laid hands on a blind man more than once and not all of His healings happened immediately (see Mark 8:22-25 and Luke 17:11-19, for example).

If you have laid hands on a person a couple of times and the healing has not started to manifest after a couple of days, there may be an afflicting spirit which is preventing the healing. Ask God to reveal to you what kind of spirit is causing the person's infirmity and then cast it out. Also, there might be spiritual interference in the place where you are ministering healing, which can prevent the healing unless you deal with the spiritual interference or move to another place.

Another thing to consider is that God might not want to heal the person by the laying-on of hands. When Lazarus was sick, it was not God's will for Jesus to lay hands on Lazarus and heal him, it was God's will for Jesus to raise Lazarus from the dead (John 11:1-45). Or consider a person with clogged arteries. God could sovereignly heal the person, but if the person does not change his eating and exercising habits then the condition might return. God might want the person to visit his doctor and learn that he needs to go on a diet and exercise program. It is God's will for us to walk in health, but this does not always mean that He will miraculously heal everyone by the laying-on of hands. As always, be sensitive to the leading of the Holy Spirit concerning the way in which God wants to heal the person.

Sometimes a person doesn't get healed simply because his faith or your faith is not strong enough for that healing. It is important to show people from Scripture that healing is for today and sometimes it helps for people to see a healing with their own eyes so that their faith will rise for their own healing. Again, it is also very helpful to talk to the person about his theological problems concerning healing and his fears and doubts about healing. After you deal with these fears and doubts and theological problems, you will often find that the person easily receives his healing. However, since our faith is never going to be perfect, there may be times when we need to go to the doctor and have surgery or go on medication. None of us understands everything about healing, so if our healing is not manifesting for some reason then we should see a doctor.

Make sure that the person actually *wants* to be healed! Jesus asked a man at the pool of Bethesda if he wanted to get well (John 5:6) and we should do the same if nothing seems to be happening. Under most circumstances you will not be able to cast out demons or minister healing if the person does not want to let go of these things.

Sometimes people are not healed because there is unconfessed sin in their lives. If you have done all that you know to do and you are not seeing results, ask God for guidance and listen to what the Holy Spirit tells you. If the Spirit reveals a word or an impression to you about unforgiveness, unconfessed sin, etc., in the person's heart then gently and sensitively ask about these things and then deal with them appropriately (through prayer, confessing the sins, forgiving someone, etc.).

Warning: Always be very discreet with personal information that the Holy Spirit gives you about people! Under no circumstances should you share this information with anyone else. If God wants other people to know this information then let *God* reveal it to them, because it would be very harmful for you to share the information with anyone else and it will damage the trust that God wants to have in you!

Be very careful not to put condemnation on the person by making him feel that it's *his* fault he's not getting healed.

Another thing you can do is to read this Healing Book again in case there is some information that you have overlooked or have forgotten about.

The Healing Power of GodLULUjacket

Also read other books on healing such as the ones listed in the next section.

Continuing Study

We must never stop searching for new ways to walk in healing. After reading this Book you now have enough information to begin laying hands on the sick. As you remain teachable and humble and open to the Holy Spirit, He will teach you more and more about healing. When He teaches you new things about healing, teach them to others!

May the Lord richly bless your life with fruitfulness for the Kingdom as you go out and continue His evangelism and healing ministry and as you train others to do the same until He returns.

YOU can heal the sick in Jesus' Name!

The New Testament never says that it is God's will for us to remain sick or injured or disabled. Instead, the New Testament consistently shows that healing and health are God's will for us (as we will see). This does not mean that everyone will always be healed (for reasons which we will see later), but the more we understand what the New Testament says about healing, the more likely it is that we will receive the healing that we need!

Healing Faith

We must have faith for healing. The first thing to understand is that healing comes *by faith*. In this article you'll learn some ways of putting your faith into *action* to help you receive your healing.

But where does faith come from? Here is God's answer: "*faith comes from hearing the message*, and the message is heard *through the word of Christ*." (Romans 10:17)

This says that faith comes from *hearing the message through the word of Christ*.

Therefore, every time you come across a Scripture passage in this article, read it out loud several times so that you are *hearing God's Word*. You see, faith is not an emotion, as many people think. Faith involves a *decision* and an *action*.

So make the decision that you are going to act on faith by reading each passage out loud, pondering it, chewing on it, getting the meaning of it, letting it really sink in. God says that this will develop faith in you.

Now, read the following passages out loud and see if you can spot the one common thing which helped these people receive their healing: "Some men brought to him a paralytic, Laid on a mat. When Jesus *saw their faith*, he said to the paralytic, ... "Get up, take your mat and go home." *And the man got up* and went home." (Matthew 9:2-7)

"*By faith* in the name of Jesus, this man whom you see and know was made strong. It is Jesus' name *and the faith* that comes through him that has given this complete healing to him, as you can all see." (Acts 3:16)

"In Lystra there sat a man crippled in his feet, who was lame from birth and had never walked. He listened to Paul as he was speaking. Paul looked directly at him, *saw that he had faith to be healed* and called out, "Stand up on your feet!" At that, *the man jumped up* and began to walk." (Acts 14:8-10)

"Then he touched their eyes and said, "*According to your faith* will it be done to you"; and their sight was restored." (Matthew 9:29-30) "What do you want me to do for you?" Jesus asked him. The blind man said, "Rabbi, I want to see." "Go," said Jesus, "*your faith has healed you*." Immediately he received his sight and followed Jesus along the road. (Mark 10:51-52)

Then he said to her, "Daughter, *your faith has healed you*." (Luke 8:48)

Then he said to him, "Rise and go; *your faith has made you well*."(Luke 17:19)

Notice that *their faith* was involved in receiving their healing!

Think of faith as being kind of like a pipeline. If that "pipeline" is clogged by your doubt and unbelief then it can hinder God's healing power from flowing into you. Your faith helps keep the pipeline open (so to speak).

Your faith helps bring the healing to you, so it's important to know how to use your faith in order to open up that pipeline and receive the healing into your body.

Healing is God's Will

This has been something I've heard many say, Lord if it be your will. In order to have faith for your healing, it is important to get it settled in your heart that healing and health are God's will for us. This doesn't mean that we will always receive the healing that we want, because in this article we will see that there are things which can hinder our healing. My point is simply that the New Testament never says that it is God's will for a person to remain sick or injured or disabled, but instead the New Testament consistently shows that healing and health are God's will for us.

For example, notice that while Jesus was on the earth, God the Father was accomplishing His *will* through Jesus: Jesus answered: "Don't you know me, Philip, even after I have been among you such a long time? *Anyone who has seen me has seen the Father.* How can you say, 'Show us the Father'? Don't you believe that *I am in the Father, and that the Father is in me*? The words I say to you are not just my own. Rather, *it is the Father, living in me, who is doing his work.*" (John 14:9-10)

As you repeat this passage out loud several times, think about what it means. It means that when we see Jesus doing things in the Bible, *those things are God's will*.

People sometimes wonder whether or not healing and health are God's will for us, so let's look at how Jesus answered this question: "*A man with leprosy* came and knelt before him and said, "*Lord, if you are willing, you can make me clean.*" Jesus reached out his hand and touched the man. "*I am willing*," he said. "Be clean!" Immediately he was cured of his leprosy." (Matthew 8:2-3)

As you repeat this passage out loud, think about this: Was Jesus willing to heal back then? Yes! Therefore, it was *God's will* to heal people back then. But is Jesus still willing to give us healing today? Yes! Jesus Christ is the *same* yesterday and today and forever: "Jesus Christ is the *same* yesterday and today and forever." (Hebrews 13:8)

As you repeat this passage out loud (building faith for your healing), let it sink in that *Jesus does not change*. He was the Healer back then and He is still the Healer today. Jesus does the will of God the Father, so healing and health are God's will for us. Sometimes a healing might happen instantly and sometimes you will need to exercise patience until you see the healing and sometimes you might not receive healing at all for one reason or another (later we'll see some reasons why).

Remember that Jesus healed everyone who wanted healing, which shows that healing and health are God's will for *everyone*.

There is not a single case in the New Testament where anyone who wanted divine healing did not receive it and there is not a single case where a person was told that his sickness was for the purpose of building character in him and there is not a single case where sickness was called a "blessing" and there is not a single case where a sick person who wanted healing was left unhealed for any reason (this includes Lazarus, because Jesus resurrected him back to life and health) and there is not a single case where God used a sickness to bring someone Home to heaven and there is not a single case where a person was told that it was not God's will for him to be healed and there is not a single case where Jesus said that sickness glorifies God (it is *healing* that glorifies God) and there is not a single case where Jesus said that God had put sickness on someone to punish him or to chastise him and there is not a single case where Jesus told people to be patient in sickness and so on.

The point here is that Jesus healed *everyone* who came to Him for healing and He is the *same* yesterday and today and forever.

Let it sink into your heart, let it become *real* to you that healing and health are God's will. Get this settled in your heart so that you have faith for your healing!

Already Been Paid For

In order to have faith for your healing, it is also important to get it settled in your heart that your healing has *already* been paid for. You don't have to earn it; it is a *free gift* from God to you! You simply have to *receive* it by properly using your faith.

Notice what the prophet Isaiah said: "Surely *our sicknesses he hath borne, And our pains -- he hath carried them*, And we -- we have esteemed him plagued, Smitten of God, and afflicted. And he is pierced for our transgressions, Bruised for our iniquities, The chastisement of our peace *is* on him, *And by his bruise there is healing to us*. ... *And he the sin of many hath borne*" (Isaiah 53:4-5, 12, Young's Literal Translation)

Repeat this passage several times, out loud. Speaking prophetically about Jesus, Isaiah said, "our *sicknesses* he *hath borne* [taken away]," and then Isaiah said, "he the *sin* of many *hath borne* [taken away]." Notice the similarity in these statements. Just as Jesus took away all of our sins, He also took away all of our sicknesses and infirmities.

Jesus gives us salvation as a free gift by faith and He also gives us healing as a free gift by faith!

In the New Testament, the apostle Peter quoted from Isaiah's prophecy: "He himself *bore our sins* in his body on the tree, so that we might die to sins and live for righteousness; *by his wounds you have been healed*." (1 Peter 2:24)

As you repeat this passage several times, hearing God's Word so that it builds faith in you, let it sink in that Jesus paid for our sins *and* He paid for our healing. Many sincere, well-meaning Christians believe that the above passage refers to "spiritual healing," which they interpret as being salvation.

Now notice the tense of the verbs in (1 Peter 2:24 above). They are in the *past tense*.

The prophet Isaiah was looking ahead to what Jesus was going to do for us on the cross and the apostle Peter was looking *back* to what Jesus has *already done* for us on the cross. It is done! Our sins are paid for and our healing needs are paid for. Jesus did His part in purchasing your healing and now you have a part to play in receiving your healing, because people usually don't *automatically* get healed. Here are several examples from the Bible to show you what I mean: "Then [Jesus] said to the man, "*Stretch out your hand.*" So *he stretched it out and it was completely restored, just as sound as the other.*" (Matthew 12:13)

[Jesus] said to the paralyzed man, "I tell you, *get up, take your mat and go home.*" Immediately *he stood up* in front of them, took what he had laid on and went home praising God. (Luke 5:24-25)

"Then Jesus said to him, "*Get up! Pick up your mat and walk.*" At once *the man was cured; he picked up his mat and walked.*" (John 5:8-9)

"Go," [Jesus] told him, "*wash in the Pool of Siloam*" (this word means Sent). *So the man went and washed, and came home seeing.* (John 9:7)

"As he was going into a village, ten men who had leprosy met him. They stood at a distance and called out in a loud voice, "Jesus, Master, have pity on us!" When he saw them, he said, "*Go, show yourselves to the priests.*" And *as they went, they were cleansed.*" (Luke 17:12-14)

In the above passages, notice that the man with the shriveled hand had to *decide* to stretch out his hand. Some crippled people had to *decide* to get up onto their feet. A blind man had to *decide* to wash in the Pool of Siloam. Some lepers had to *decide* to go show themselves to the priests. That's how they put their faith into *action*. By the way, notice that the blind man and the 10 lepers were not instantly healed. The blind man was healed when he washed in the Pool of Siloam and the 10 lepers were healed on their way to the city where the priests were located. In the same way, it's possible that you might not instantly receive healing either. You might receive your healing as you go about your daily business, taking Jesus at His word and staying in faith (keeping your "pipeline" open), patiently waiting until the healing is complete.

Doubt, and Unbelief Can Hinder Your Faith

This is the worst things I've seen in the Church, doubt and unbelief. So far we have seen that healing often requires *faith*. If we have fear, doubt, or unbelief in our minds, it can *hinder* our faith (it clogs up our "pipeline," so to speak).

To show you what I mean, notice that Peter (a normal man) walked on water by faith: "Lord, if it's you," Peter replied, "tell me to come to you on the water." "Come," he said. Then *Peter got down out of the boat, walked on the water* and came toward Jesus.

But when he saw the wind, he was afraid and, beginning to sink, cried out, "Lord, save me!"
Immediately Jesus reached out his hand and caught him. "You of little faith," he said, "*why did you doubt?*"(Matthew 14:28-31)

As you repeat this passage out loud, really ponder on what was going on here. Notice that as long as Peter kept his eyes on Jesus, he did the impossible: He walked on top of the water. But when he took his eyes off of Jesus and saw the wind and the waves, he allowed fear and doubt to come into his mind.

Then he sank like a rock! The wind and the waves were there the whole time, but the key factor was the choice that Peter made with his mind. When he *chose* to keep his eyes on Jesus, a miracle happened.

When he *allowed* fear and doubt into his mind, it canceled out the miracle. What this means is that the battle for your miracle takes place in your mind!

The wind and the waves were always there, but it was what Peter *focused on* that made all the difference in the world.

Here's how that applies to healing. Yes, you might have pain. Yes, you might have symptoms of disease. I'm not suggesting that you pretend they don't exist. Your symptoms are real and if you need to take medicine, take medicine. If you need to go to the doctor, go to the doctor.

If you need to schedule surgery, schedule surgery (and stay in faith that your healing might be complete before the surgery date). But remember, Peter stayed in faith by focusing on Jesus.

He lost the battle for faith when he focused on the wind and the waves. Your symptoms are real, but you need to focus on Jesus and the healing that He has bought for you, rather than focusing on your symptoms.

The Bible says, "We live by faith, *not* by sight" (2 Corinthians 5:7). Focus on maintaining your faith in Jesus, don't focus on what you see or feel. You can do this by continually thanking Him for your healing, praising Him for your healing, reading and memorizing and speaking Scripture passages on healing (remember, faith comes from *hearing* the Word of God) and so on.

Notice what the Bible says: "*Everything is possible for him who believes.*" (Mark 9:23)

"*But when he asks, he must believe and not doubt*, because *he who doubts* is like a wave of the sea, blown and tossed by the wind. *That man should not think he will receive anything from the Lord*" (James 1:6-7)

"Therefore I tell you, *whatever* you ask for in prayer, *believe that you have received it, and it will be yours*." (Mark 11:24)

Read these passages carefully several times, out loud. Think about what God is telling us. Remember, God does not lie and He says that *everything* is possible for us *if we believe*. He says that we must believe *and not doubt*, because fear, doubt and unbelief can hinder our faith.

If we accept the doubts that the devil tries to put into our minds, then we should not expect to receive anything from the Lord (James 1:6-7, above). See how important it is to stay in faith and to banish all fear, doubt and unbelief from our minds? The battle takes place in your mind and your mind can hinder you from receiving divine healing.

The third passage above (Mark 11:24) gives us the key to receiving from God. We must *first* believe that we have received whatever we ask for (such as healing) and *then* we will receive it. See the order there? People tend to say, "I'll believe it when I see it," but God tells us that we will see it *if* we believe it first.

When your questions about divine healing are adequately answered then it will enable you to begin removing doubts from your mind which might be canceling out your faith for healing.

Sometimes people have tried to believe for something but they never received it, so they don't like it when people teach this "faith" stuff. But remember that it's *God* who places such a heavy emphasis on faith!

Often the problem is simply that these sincere, well-meaning Christians have not fully understood how faith works, or they were not aware of things that can hinder our healing. Remember, if we want to get God's results (such as divine healing) then we've got to do it God's way. Consider that if you speak a lie often enough then you begin to believe it, right?

So begin speaking the Truth (God's Word) often enough until you really believe it! God says that this is how faith can be developed (Romans 10:17). If you have too many doubts about divine healing then you shouldn't expect to receive it (James 1:6-7 and Mark 11:24, above).

You need to decide for yourself if God was telling the truth or if He was lying in the above passages. If we believe that He was telling the truth, then we've got to do what He says!

Receiving Your Healing

This is a day we all need to learn how to receive healing. Okay, now it's time to get specific. What can you *do* to receive divine healing?

It is important for you to continually make the choice not to doubt and not to fear. For example, when the doctor says "cancer," our natural reaction is to become afraid. But remember, God is *bigger* than all of our problems put together! God made these bodies of ours and He can fix *anything* that goes wrong with them. Therefore, when you get a "bad report" from the doctor, *don't accept it*! In your mind say, "I don't receive that."

If you allow that "bad report" to get down into your heart then it will be difficult to have faith for your healing (for example, "as he thinketh in his heart, so is he" - Proverbs 23:7). Don't accept defeat! Don't accept a negative attitude or a negative viewpoint! If the doctor says that you need more tests or you need medication or whatever, follow your doctor's orders. You are under his or her authority. But don't receive the "bad report" down inside of you because it will become a root of fear or doubt within you. Watch what Jesus did when a man received a "bad report" that his daughter had died: "While Jesus was still speaking, some men came from the house of Jairus, the synagogue ruler. "*Your daughter is dead,*" they said. "Why bother the teacher any more?"

Ignoring what they said, Jesus told the synagogue ruler, "*Don't be afraid; just believe.*" (Mark 5:35-36)

Notice that Jesus *ignored* the bad report and he specifically told the dead girl's father to believe and not to fear. That's what you need to do. Follow your doctor's orders, but disregard the "bad report" that your doctor and your body (and your family members) are giving you. Your job is to believe and not to fear.

Yes, you have real symptoms in your body, but those symptoms are not the *truth*. For example, I am a Christian, I am saved. But sometimes when I get up in the morning I don't *feel* very saved until I have a cup of coffee. Notice that my salvation is based on what Jesus has already done for me, it is not based on how I *feel*. My feelings are real, but they are not the truth.

In the same way, your healing is based on what Jesus has *already done* for you, so don't focus on your symptoms or how you "feel." Your feelings are real, but they are not the truth. The Word of God is the truth and we need to trust it!

It is also important to understand the difference between *faith* and *hope*. Hope is always looking to the future. Faith is always *now*. For example, take a look at what the Bible says about faith: "*Now faith is being sure* of what we hope for and *certain* of what we do not see." (Hebrews 11:1)

As Bible commentators have pointed out, this verse means that faith is like the "title-deed" which we own as a current reality while we are waiting for the things hoped for: [The Greek word for "being sure"] is common in the [ancient] papyri in business documents *as the basis or guarantee of transactions*. "And as this is the essential meaning in (Hebrews 11:1) we venture to suggest the translation *Faith is the title-deed* of things hoped for"

"[Faith] substantiates promises of God which we hope for, as future in fulfillment, making them *present realities* to us.... Through faith, the future object of Christian hope, *in its beginning*, is *already present*. True faith infers the *reality* of the objects believed in and hoped for (Hebrews 11:6). By *faith* alone we are sure of eternal things *that they ARE*: but by *hope* we are confident that WE SHALL HAVE them. All hope presupposes faith (Romans 8:25)."

So faith is in the present tense, such as, "Healing is mine *right now*, because Jesus has already paid for my healing and I am expectantly waiting for it to arrive."

Here's an illustration to make this clearer. Imagine that your uncle orders a book for you as a birthday gift, to be delivered to your house. His credit card was charged for the book, but for some reason it never arrived on your doorstep. If you call the company, you might say something like, "That book has been *paid for* and it is *mine*. I *expect* you to send it to me." You are already thinking of the book as *yours* because it has been paid for and it has been given to you as a gift, even though it has not yet been delivered to you. See the analogy?

Jesus has already paid for your healing and He has given it to you as a free gift. As soon as you decide to accept the gift, it is *yours*. Healing is now yours, *even if you have no evidence of it yet*, just like you consider the book to be yours even before it is delivered to you. Your job is to patiently wait for the healing to be delivered to your body, *expecting* that it will eventually come because it has been bought and paid for and it is yours. For example, if you are a Christian then you have faith that you will go to heaven. You *expect* that you will go to heaven some day. So faith sometimes involves expectantly waiting.

Another thing to consider is that the devil and his demons can put sicknesses and infirmities on us: "On a Sabbath Jesus was teaching in one of the synagogues and *a woman was there who had been crippled by a spirit for eighteen years. She was bent over and could not straighten up at all*. When Jesus saw her, he called her forward and said to her, "Woman, you are set free from your infirmity." Then he put his hands on her and immediately she straightened up and praised God." (Luke 13:10-13)

When Jesus saw that a crowd was running to the scene, he rebuked the evil spirit. *"You deaf and mute spirit,"* he *said, "I command you, come out of him and never enter him again."* (Mark 9:25)

You won't always know if a demon is causing your sickness, but if there is a demon at work then you probably won't be able to receive your healing until you cast out that afflicting spirit. As you probably know, some of the wrong things that we or our ancestors have done (or some of the wrong things that have been done to us) can open the door for the devil to attack us and this procedure might help to break those attacks. After I wrote this Book, I went through the procedure myself. I didn't feel anything happen, but later I realized that I was no longer struggling against various improper thoughts. I believe that I had freed myself from a spirit that I never knew was there.

Also, our sins can sometimes hinder us from receiving healing. The article above will help you to confess your sins and receive forgiveness.

Now let's talk about instant miracles of healing. We all want that, right? In the New Testament, Jesus laid hands on lots of sick people and He saw lots of instant miracles of healing. Then He said that *anyone who has faith in Him* can do the *same* miracles that He did. In fact, He specifically said that *those who believe* will *lay hands on the sick*: "the people brought to Jesus all who had various kinds of sickness, and *laying his hands on each one, he healed them*." (Luke 4:40)

"at least believe on the evidence of the *miracles* themselves. I tell you the truth, *anyone who has faith in me will do what I have been doing*." (John 14:11-12)

"And these signs will accompany *those who believe*: ... *they will place their hands on sick people, and they will get well.*" (Mark 16:17-18)

This means that you can find a Christian who understands about laying hands on the sick and ask that person to lay hands on you. I have seen cancer instantly healed, back pain instantly healed, a broken and improperly-healed jaw instantly healed, short arms and legs instantly growing out, a person with no peripheral vision instantly healed and so on when I have laid hands on people (I have also seen nothing happen when I have laid hands on people). Consider looking in your local phone book for some non-denominational charismatic churches in your area, then call them to see if they have a healing and deliverance ministry. Many of them do, in which case they will probably be happy to lay hands on you and pray for you.

Consider that all of the sick people in the New Testament had to *wait* before they received their "instant" miracles of healing.

People had to wait for Jesus to walk up to them, or they had to wait to be carried to Jesus, or they had to wait their turn while Jesus laid His hands on people in the crowds (as in Luke 4:40, above) and so on. Even though we tend to say that people received instant miracles of healing in the New Testament, the truth is that they all had to *wait* until Jesus was near them or until He spoke the healing for them. In a similar way, you will need to wait until that moment when you "instantly" receive your healing and it is important that your waiting is done patiently and expectantly, without grumbling or complaining.

We don't always know why it sometimes takes so long for our healing to arrive, but in the spiritual realm there are things going on that we can't always see. Here's an example: "Then {the angel} said to me, Fear not, Daniel, for from *the first day* that you set your mind *and* heart to understand and to humble yourself before your God, *your words were heard, and I have come in consequence of your words*. But the prince {the territorial demon} of the kingdom of Persia *withstood me for twenty-one days*. But Michael {the archangel Michael}, one of the chief *of the celestial princes*, came to help me" (Daniel 10:12-13, AMP.)

Here we see that a man named Daniel was praying for something. On the *first* day that he began praying, an angel was sent to him with the answer.

However, there was a heavenly battle which prevented this angel from reaching Daniel right away. Daniel remained patient and continued to pray for 21 days and finally the angel arrived with the answer to Daniel's prayer. We don't always know why it sometimes takes so long for our healing to get here, but our job is to stay in faith and to remain patient, no matter how long it takes.

Unfortunately, this is where we tend to fall apart. We get tired of waiting and then we allow doubts into our minds, which hinder our faith: "But when he asks, *he must believe and not doubt*, because *he who doubts* is like a wave of the sea, blown and tossed by the wind. *That man should not think he will receive anything from the Lord*; he is a double-minded man, unstable in all he does." (James 1:6-8)

It is important for us to get control of our minds and stay patient so that we keep that "pipeline" of faith open for as long as it takes.

If we need to get control of our minds then how do we do that?

We saw earlier that faith comes from *hearing God's Word* (Romans 10:17). When you speak in line with what God says, it builds faith within you even if you don't "feel" it. Take a look at what the Bible says:

"Do not let this Book of the Law depart from your mouth; meditate on it day and night, so that you may be careful to do everything written in it. *Then* you will be prosperous and successful." (Joshua 1:8)

"I will *remember* the deeds of the LORD; yes, I will *remember* your miracles of long ago. I will *meditate* on all your works and *consider* all your mighty deeds." (Psalms 77:11-12)

"*With my lips* I recount all the laws that come from your mouth. I *rejoice* in following your statutes as one rejoices in great riches. I *meditate* on your precepts and *consider* your ways. I *delight* in your decrees; *I will not neglect your word*." (Psalms 119:13-16)

In order to get control of our minds, it is helpful to "meditate" on the things that God says (as in the passages above, not as in some kind of New Age meditation).

According to Strong's Hebrew Dictionary, the Hebrew words for "meditate" in the above passages mean "murmur," "ponder," "imagine," "meditate," "mutter," "study," "utter," "converse," "declare," "muse," "pray," "talk," "speak." Faith comes from *hearing* what God says (Romans 10:17) and we are told to *meditate* on what God says, so when we read what God says about healing, when we study what God says about healing, when we speak what God says about healing, when we ponder what God says about healing, when we rejoice in what God says about healing, when we remember past healings and so on, then we are building faith for our healing.

The more we speak the Word of God and speak words of faith and saturate our minds with the things that God says about healing, the more we are preventing doubts and fears from being able to enter our minds. Are you speaking faith words or doubt words? Conquering words or fear words? Healing words or sickness words? Positive words or negative, complaining words? It's time to cut out all of the "pity parties" and the complaining and the negative talk and instead saturate your mind and your words with the things that God says and with praises and thanksgiving.

Here's an example from the Bible where a woman used some of these principles to receive her healing: "So Jesus went with him. *A large crowd followed and pressed around him.* And a woman was there who had been subject to bleeding for twelve years. ... When she heard about Jesus, she came up behind him in the crowd and touched his cloak, because she thought [literally, "*she said to herself*" - see Matthew 9:21], "*If I just touch his clothes, I will be healed.*" Immediately her bleeding stopped and she felt in her body that she was freed from her suffering. At once Jesus realized that power had gone out from him. He turned around in the crowd and asked, "Who touched my clothes?" "*You see the people crowding against you,*" *his disciples answered,* "*and yet you can ask, Who touched me?*"

But Jesus kept looking around to see who had done it. Then the woman, knowing what had happened to her, came and fell at his feet and trembling with fear, told him the whole truth. He said to her, "Daughter, *your faith has healed you*. Go in peace and be freed from your suffering." (Mark 5:24-34)

This woman *said to herself*, "If I just touch his clothes, I will be healed." Notice that she was focusing on Jesus, "meditating" on God's healing power and pushing doubt and fear from her mind by speaking words of faith. Many other people were touching Jesus, but the Bible does not mention anyone else being healed here. This woman is being singled out in this passage in order to describe how she received her healing. Jesus said that it was *her faith* which had healed her.

Now take a look at the following passages: "I tell you the *truth*, if anyone *says to this mountain*, 'Go, throw yourself into the sea,' and *does not doubt* in his heart but *believes that what he says will happen*, it will be done for him." (Mark 11:23)

"Seeing a fig tree by the road, he went up to it but found nothing on it except leaves. Then *he said to it*, "May you never bear fruit again!" *Immediately the tree withered*. When the disciples saw this, they were amazed. "How did the fig tree wither so quickly?" they asked. Jesus replied, "I tell you the *truth*, *if you have faith and do not doubt*, not only can *you* do what was done to the fig tree, but also *you can say to this mountain*, 'Go, throw yourself into the sea,' and it *will* be done. *If you believe, you will receive whatever you ask for in prayer*." (Matthew 21:19-22)

"I tell you the *truth*, *if you have faith* as small as a mustard seed, *you can say to this mountain*, 'Move from here to there' and it *will* move. *Nothing will be impossible for you*." (Matthew 17:20)

He replied, "*If you have faith* as small as a mustard seed, *you can say to this mulberry tree*, 'Be uprooted and planted in the sea,' and *it will obey you*." (Luke 17:6)

Jesus says that *we* can command fig trees and mulberry trees and mountains. Is He giving us lessons about gardening and telling us to re-arrange mountain ranges? No, He is teaching us principles of faith.

He is talking to *us* in these passages (if we have faith), so watch what happens when we plug our names into these Scripture passages. Here's how they look with my name: "I tell you the *truth, if Bill says to this mountain*, 'Go, throw yourself into the sea,' and *does not doubt* in his heart but *believes that what he says will happen*, it will be done *for Bill*." (Mark 11:23)

Jesus replied, "I tell you the *truth, if Bill has faith and does not doubt*, not only can *Bill* do what was done to the fig tree, but also *Bill can say to this mountain*, 'Go, throw yourself into the sea,' and it *will* be done. *If Bill believes, Bill will receive whatever he asks for in prayer.*" (Matthew 21:21-22)

"I tell you the *truth, if Bill has faith* as small as a mustard seed, *Bill can say to this mountain*, 'Move from here to there' and it *will* move. *Nothing will be impossible for Bill.*" (Matthew 17:20)

He replied, "*If Bill has faith* as small as a mustard seed, *Bill can say to this mulberry tree*, 'Be uprooted and planted in the sea,' and *it will obey Bill.*" (Luke 17:6)

Jesus is speaking to *you* as well, so read these passages with *your* name! Do you see what He is saying? Jesus is not telling us to talk *about* the mountains in our lives (mountains of sickness and so on), He is telling us to talk *to* the mountains in our lives and *command* them to go! It is good to have other people praying for you, but if you are able to speak then it is important for *you* to talk to your mountain and tell it to jump into the sea.

It is important for *you* to curse your sickness and command it to die (like the fig tree in the passage above).

So here's what you can do. Whenever you experience doubts, unbelief, fear, etc., don't let those things hinder your healing! Fight back! For example, you can say something like this: "Lord Jesus, I thank You that You have paid for all of my healing needs. As it is written in (Isaiah 53:4-5) and (Matthew 8:17), You took up all of my infirmities and pains and sicknesses. As it is written in (1 Peter 2:24), by Your stripes I am healed. You have given me healing as a free gift and on October 16, 2000 [put your date here], I accepted that free gift with joy and thankfulness. The healing that I need is now mine and I am patiently waiting as long as it takes until the healing is complete in my body.

I am standing in faith on the Word of God and I refuse to allow any fear or doubt into my mind. Devil, in Jesus' Name you take that cancer [or whatever it is] off of my body because I'm not signing for that package. Cancer [or whatever it is], you have no legal right to attack my body because Jesus has already purchased my healing and I have received my healing by faith. You are a mountain and as it is written in (Mark 11:23) I take authority over you in Jesus' Name and I command you to leave my body now. Get off of me and be cast into the sea! I rebuke you, as it is written in (Luke 4:39). I curse you at the roots and command you to die in Jesus' Name, as it is written in (Mark 11:20-24). Lord, I am confessing that You are my Healer and I thank You for Your healing power that is working in my body right now!"

Say these types of things, ponder them, meditate on them and let these things sink down deep inside of you so that they are maintaining a high level of faith in you (even if you don't *feel* anything). This isn't about "word power" or some kind of New Age meditation, this is about staying focused on Jesus and the Word of God and about keeping your faith at a high level and about banishing fears and doubts from your mind. Remember that Jesus told a man to "don't be afraid; just believe": "While Jesus was still speaking, some men came from the house of Jairus, the synagogue ruler. "*Your daughter is dead,*" they said. "Why bother the teacher any more?" *Ignoring what they said*, Jesus told the synagogue ruler, "*Don't be afraid; just believe.*" (Mark 5:35-36)

When doubts or fears come into your mind, that's your signal that the devil might be trying to attack you and steal your healing (see John 10:10 and Ephesians 6:16-17). Right away you need to begin saying some words of praise and words of faith so that you are resisting the devil (see James 4:7) and so that you are pushing the doubts and fears out of your mind. Faith is a *fight* (see 1 Timothy 6:2) and the battle is won or lost in your mind. You can choose to live by faith (and not by sight - 2 Corinthians 5:7), or you can choose to have "pity parties" and complain about your situation. Your choice will either help or hinder receiving your healing.

Another thing you can do is to pray for other people who need healing: "pray for each other so that *you* may be healed." (James 5:16)

When you pray for other people who need healing, it's like you are sowing seeds for a harvest of healing to meet your own needs. Remember, "A man reaps what he sows" (Galatians 6:7). Stay in faith that as you sow seeds of prayer for others, the harvest that you need is working in you.

Remember that you are responsible for taking care of your body. If you are not getting enough sleep, if you are not getting enough exercise, if you are not eating properly, etc., then your body will not function at its best and it will be less able to fight off sicknesses and diseases. This is one reason why you should go to a doctor when necessary. The doctor might tell you to quit smoking or quit drinking or begin an exercise program or change your eating habits.

For example, if God heals your clogged arteries but you do not change your ways, you'll just get clogged arteries again!

Keep in mind that after you are healed, the devil might try to put *symptoms* back on you. Don't accept them! The devil's goal is to steal and kill and destroy (John 10:10) and he might be able to steal your healing from you if you let him (see Matthew 12:43-45 and John 5:14, for example). If you start noticing symptoms again after you have received healing, you should immediately say, "Devil, I received my healing on [put your date here] and I do not accept those symptoms back on my body. In Jesus' Name you take those symptoms off of me, because I'm not signing for that package!"

Don't be timid with the devil, be aggressive and stand in the authority that Jesus died to give you. For example, think about an army general. When he gives a command, he's not wimpy about it, right? He gives commands with *authority* and he *expects* them to be obeyed!

Conclusion

Many people will refuse to do some of these things because "our church doesn't do things that way," or, "that doesn't make any sense to me," or, "I know someone who tried it and it didn't work." Then they will wonder why they are not receiving any healing. It is human nature to come up with rationalizations such as, "God must be working on my character," or, "God must be chastising me," or, "It must not be God's will for me to be healed" and so on. However, we should be careful about making rationalizations like these because if we're wrong then we are speaking words of doubt and unbelief, which can hinder our faith.

Remember, healing is not automatic. If it were automatic then there would not be any sick people in the world!

We sometimes need to *do* something in order to receive healing. It is important for us to pray, but don't we all know of people who prayed and yet they never received healing? Why is that? Perhaps they weren't quite following God's principles, or perhaps they believed some of the above rationalizations. We don't really know how much faith someone else has and we don't know if they were putting their faith into *action* and we don't know if they had doubts or fears or misconceptions about healing that hindered their faith and we don't know if they were confusing hope or desperation with faith and we don't know if they were "speaking to their mountains" or not and we don't know if they *expected* to receive their healing and we don't know if they exercised *patience* or if they gave up too soon and we don't know if they were *meditating* on God's Word and we don't know if they were having "pity parties" and speaking negative, complaining words and we don't know if they were resisting the devil with words of faith and so on. So don't base your views on other people's experiences!

Teaching about faith for healing is not meant to put condemnation on anyone who is still sick and we should remember that it was Jesus Himself who put such a great emphasis on faith. The point is, if you want God's results (such as healing), then it is important to make sure that you are doing it God's way. Study the Scriptural proof in this Book and stay open to the teaching and leading of the Holy Spirit, even if He gives you peace about things which are not taught at your church.

If your church or your spouse or your family or your friends do not have the same understanding about faith that you now have, it might not be a good idea to tell them that you are standing in faith for your healing. They might respond with doubt and unbelief which might hinder your attempts to stay in faith. Remember that Jesus did not do miracles in an atmosphere of doubt and unbelief and several times He took people *away* from doubters before healing them (see Mark 6:2-6, 5:38-42, 7:32-35 and 8:22-25, for example).

About the Author

Bill Vincent is no stranger to understanding the power of God. Not only has he spent over twenty years as a Minister with a strong prophetic anointing, he is now also an Apostle and Author with Revival Waves of Glory Ministries in Litchfield, IL. Along with his wife, Tabitha, he, leads a team providing apostolic oversight in all aspects of ministry, including service, personal ministry and Godly character.

Bill offers a wide range of writings and teachings from deliverance, to experiencing presence of God and developing Apostolic cutting edge Church structure. Drawing on the power of the Holy Spirit through years of experience in Revival, Spiritual Sensitivity, and deliverance ministry, Bill now focuses mainly on pursuing the Presence of God and breaking the power of the devil off of people's lives.

His books 48 and counting has since helped many people to overcome the spirits and curses of Satan. For more information or to keep up with Bill's latest releases, please visit www.revivalwavesofgloryministries.com. To contact Bill, feel free to follow him on twitter @revivalwaves.

Recommended Books

By Bill Vincent
Overcoming Obstacles
Glory: Pursuing God's Presence
Defeating the Demonic Realm
Increasing Your Prophetic Gift
Increasing Your Anointing
Keys to Receiving Your Miracle
The Supernatural Realm
Waves of Revival
Increase of Revelation and Restoration
The Resurrection Power of God
Discerning Your Call of God
Apostolic Breakthrough
Glory: Increasing God's Presence
Love is Waiting – Don't Let Love Pass You By
The Healing Power of God
Glory: Expanding God's Presence
Receiving Personal Prophecy
Signs and Wonders
Signs and Wonders Revelations
Children Stories
The Rapture
The Secret Place of God's Power
Building a Prototype Church
Breakthrough of Spiritual Strongholds
Glory: Revival Presence of God
Overcoming the Power of Lust
Glory: Kingdom Presence of God
Transitioning Into a Prototype Church
The Stronghold of Jezebel
Healing After Divorce
A Closer Relationship With God
Cover Up and Save Yourself

The Healing Power of GodLULUjacket

Desperate for God's Presence
The War for Spiritual Battles
Spiritual Leadership
Global Warning
Millions of Churches
Destroying the Jezebel Spirit
Awakening of Miracles
Deception and Consequences Revealed
Are You a Follower of Christ
Don't Let the Enemy Steal from You!
A Godly Shaking
The Unsearchable Riches of Christ
Heaven's Court System
Satan's Open Doors
Armed for Battle
The Wrestler
Spiritual Warfare: Complete Collection
Growing In the Prophetic
The Prototype Church: Complete Edition
Faith
The Rapture

To Order:

Email:
rwgcontact@yahoo.com

Web Site:
www.revivalwavesofgloryministries.com

The Healing Power of GodLULUjacket

Mail Order:
Revival Waves of Glory
PO Box 596
Litchfield, IL 62056

Shipping $5.00
If you mail an order and pay by check, make check out to Revival Waves of Glory.

Most books are in multiple formats such as Hardcover, Soft-Cover, Ebook (such as Kindle & Nook), and Audio Books.

The Healing Power of God

www.ingramcontent.com/pod-product-compliance
Lightning Source LLC
Chambersburg PA
CBHW052106070526
44584CB00017B/2356